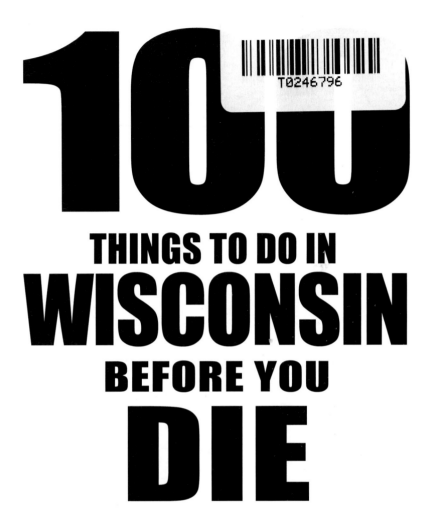

100

THINGS TO DO IN
WISCONSIN
BEFORE YOU
DIE

Step Back in Time at Heritage Hill (page 118)

100
THINGS TO DO IN
WISCONSIN
BEFORE YOU
DIE

• •

DANNELLE GAY

Copyright © 2023 by Reedy Press, LLC
Reedy Press
PO Box 5131
St. Louis, MO 63139, USA
www.reedypress.com

Library of Congress Control Number: 2022949024

ISBN: 9781681064192

Design by Jill Halpin

All photos are by the author unless otherwise noted.

Printed in the United States of America
24 25 26 27   5 4 3

DEDICATION

I want to dedicate this book to my momma—who helped
make everything a grand adventure. I miss you . . .
And to my family, who either put up with being dragged
along on these adventures or held down the homestead
while I was away. I love you ~

CONTENTS

• •

Music and Entertainment

• •

Sports and Recreation

• •

Culture and History

Shopping and Fashion

PREFACE

Nestled in the heart of the Midwest, Wisconsin is often referred to as "The Badger State." It's a land of rolling hills and picturesque farmland, renowned for its production of dairy, lumber, and beer, and also for its fishing.

But there's more to Wisconsin than meets the eye. Beneath its rural exterior lies a deep and eventful history waiting to be discovered. Nature-lovers will find plenty of parks to explore, with miles of hiking trails winding through sandstone cliffs and icy caves. And for those seeking a more urban experience, many cities offer museums, an array of cultural and artistic attractions, and more.

This multicultural melting pot encompasses everything from 11 tribes of Native Americans to Germans, Swedes, English, French, Irish, Polish, Finns, and Norwegians. We continue embracing diversity to this day, and all of it is reflected in our food, culture, and heritage.

I learned about a lot of those things on my own journeys as I grew up in a single-parent household with an amazing mother. She tried to help us find the magic in everything and planned our many adventures long before the internet could have made things easier. Day trips to places that made learning fun and included amazing places to eat became special treats that we looked forward to.

· ·

We never heard the phrase "I'll take the kids when they are older," as she figured out that there would never be a better time than the here and now.

She found the fun in the ordinary and taught us to do the same. To this day, I carry on that tradition with my own kid. We are building memories as we try new things, meet amazing people, and learn so much.

While I could easily have written a book on 1,000 things to do in Wisconsin, I had to narrow it down on my adventures across the state as I visited so many communities. I can't adequately thank the local guides who helped me on this adventure—and I loved every minute I spent eating my way through this great state.

Wisconsin is a great place to live, and there are so many things to do in this beautiful state! From the bustling city of Milwaukee to the stunning Apostle Islands, Wisconsin literally has something for everyone.

I hope this book helps you create your own adventures with your family and friends, and that it helps you create the kinds of memories my mom made for me.

Check Out the Potter's Shed (page 153)

ACKNOWLEDGMENTS

There are so many people I would love to thank for their help and support during my journey to get this book completed.

Friends like Sara Broers, who helped me get this project started, and Sadie Smiley, who helped keep me focused when I would get distracted by some shiny new project. My husband and kid put up with all sorts of short-notice getaways whether they accompanied me or not, and then read over my short summaries of what we saw.

Then there were the amazing people who worked for the local convention and visitor bureaus of different cities—Susan from Janesville, Jake from Milwaukee, Erin from Fond du Lac, Nick and Elizabeth from Green Bay, Julie from Travel Wisconsin, and Michelle and Kaitlin from Washburn County. You all made my job easier and shared so many incredible gems in your communities with me.

I truly love being the Traveling Cheesehead and sharing the amazing things I discover and experience with everyone.

JONES VALLEY FARM

SPRING GREEN, WI

ITALIAN DANDELION

TUSCAN ARUGULA $3.00

SORREL $3.50

OLIVE LEAF ARUGULA $3.50

FRISEE $4.00

CARROTS $4.00

LETTUCE $4.00 EA

Dane County Farmers Market (page 24)

FOOD AND DRINK

EAT AT A WISCONSIN SUPPER CLUB
LIKE CANTAFIO'S BUCKHORN STEAKHOUSE

Wisconsin supper clubs are a staple of the state's culture and cuisine. If you've never been to one, you're in for a treat! The atmosphere is cozy and inviting, the service is friendly and knowledgeable, and the food is delicious. Most are in older, family-owned businesses and have a full bar.

Cantafio's Buckhorn Steakhouse of Beaver Dam fits the bill perfectly. The Buckhorn has been a supper club since 1978 and is owned and operated by Joe and Bobbie Jo Cantafio. Being a Gold Star Family who lost their Marine son Ryan in 2004, they offer free meals to veterans. There is veteran paraphernalia decorating the walls, and customers can bring in pictures of their favorite vets to be added to the display.

N8802 County Rd. A, Beaver Dam, 920-885-9984
cantafiosbuckhornsteakhouse.com

TIP

Keep in mind supper clubs were a post prohibition invention. They have small dining rooms that are simply decorated, and a huge variety of cocktails to enjoy over that one to two hour experience.

OTHER GREAT WISCONSIN SUPPER CLUBS

Black Otter Supper Club
503 S Nash St., Hortonville, 920-779-6975
theblackottersupperclub.com

The Del-Bar Supper Club
800 Wisconsin Dells Pkwy., Wisconsin Dells, 608-253-1861
del-bar.com

Feil's Supper Club
N8743 State Rd. 73, Randolph, 920-326-5544
feilssupperclub.com

Fredrick's Supper Club
130 Merchant Row, Milton, 608-868-2966
facebook.com/fredrickssupperclub

Green Acres
7487 State Rd. 78, Sauk City, 608-643-2305
greenacressaukprairie.com

Norwood Pines Supper Club
10171 Hwy. 70, Minocqua, 715-356-3666
norwoodpines.com

The Packing House
900 E Layton Ave., Milwaukee, 414-483-5054
packinghousemke.com

The Roxy Supper Club
571 N Main St., Oshkosh, 920-231-1980
roxysupperclub.com

EXPERIENCE A DOOR COUNTY FISH BOIL
AT THE WHITE GULL INN

Looking for an unforgettable dining experience? Look no further than the White Gull Inn in Door County, Wisconsin. Here you can enjoy a traditional fish boil, a Door County tradition that dates back to the early 1800s. During a fish boil, fresh-caught fish are boiled in a large pot with potatoes, onions, and salt. It's a fun and tasty way to experience the local cuisine of whitefish sourced from Lake Superior or Lake Michigan.

Established in 1896, the White Gull Inn Restaurant provides a warm, charming, and traditional feel each time you visit, and you will have no regrets whether going alone or with family and friends.

The real fun is the pre-dinner show, where you can watch the fish being cooked over an open fire and be entertained by the chef on duty. After the fish is done, it will be served with melted butter sprinkled over it, and some restaurants often add tartar sauce and lemon slices.

4225 Main St., Fish Creek, 920-868-3517
whitegullinn.com

OTHER DOOR COUNTY FISH BOIL LOCATIONS

Pelletier's Restaurant & Fish Boil
4199 Main St., Fish Creek, 920-868-3313
doorcountyfishboil.com

Viking Grill & Lounge
12029 State Hwy. 42, Ellison Bay, 920-854-2998

Waterfront Mary's Bar & Grill
3662 N Duluth Ave., Sturgeon Bay, 920-743-3690
waterfrontmarysbarandgrill.com

Old Post Office Restaurant
10040 Water St., Ephraim, 920-854-4034
oldpostoffice-doorcounty.com

Log Den
6626 State Hwy. 42, Egg Harbor, 920-868-3888
thelogden.com

GET A $100 HAMBURGER
AT THE JET ROOM

OK, the burgers aren't really $100 here, but they do run a special promotion where the purchase of a $100 gift certificate includes a partnership with Wisconsin Aviation.

The Jet Room gives you a $9 credit to use on any menu item you choose, and then you are treated to a 30-minute scenic airplane ride for two around Madison. It's a great way to spend an afternoon with someone you love, and it makes for a very memorable date or gift.

The Jet Room is also a great place to take kids! You have a front-row seat at a huge wall of windows that lets you watch planes take off and land as you dine, and your favorite budding pilot gets a mini-plane kit to fuel their imaginations.

(Located inside Wisconsin Aviation terminal building)
3606 Corben Ct., Madison, 608-268-5010
jetroomrestaurant.com

TIP
You have to make arrangements separately for your flight through Wisconsin Aviation in advance of your visit.

EAT FARM-TO-FORK
AT SALVATORE'S TOMATO PIES

There isn't a Farmers Market that goes by where you don't see Patrick DePula perusing and picking up the freshest gems from local farmers at around 6:30 in the morning. Since 2011, he and his wife Nichole have been serving up their unique version of pizza—New Jersey style. A true champion of supporting the local economy and loving the ability to offer the freshest of ingredients, they rely on several local farms for everything from produce to cheeses.

They originally served only pizza, but they have expanded their menu dramatically over the last dozen years and added a few more locations to the county as well.

Not only are locals fans of their food, but we also appreciate how they are always at the front of the line to help out their neighbors in need. If you find yourself overwhelmed by their menu on your first visit, go with the Fat Uncle Tony and make sure you save room for dessert!

121 E Main St., Sun Prairie, 608-318-1761
salvatorestomatopies.com

OTHER FARM-TO-FORK PLACES WE LOVE

Braise
1101 S 2nd St., Milwaukee, 414-212-8843
braiselocalfood.com

Cedar & Sage Grill House
2040 Airport Dr., Green Bay, 920-327-7911

Genisa Wine Bar
11 N Main St., Janesville, 608-728-7964
genisawinebar.com

Goodkind
2457 S Wentworth Ave., Milwaukee, 414-763-4706
goodkindbayreview.com

Graze
1 S Pinckney St., Madison, 608-251-2700
grazemadison.com

Merchant
121 S Pinckney St., Madison, 608-259-9799
merchantmadison.com

Nucleus Café
405 Water St., Eau Claire, 715-834-7777
nucleuscafe.com

Simple Café
525 Broad St., Lake Geneva, 262-248-3556
simplelakegeneva.com

The Creamery
114 Pine St., Green Bay, 920-489-8437

Wickman House
11976 Mink River Rd., Ellison Bay, 920-854-3305
wickmanhouse.com

EAT UNDER THE GOATS
AT AL JOHNSON'S

If you're looking for a unique dining experience, Al Johnson's Swedish Restaurant in Sister Bay, Wisconsin, is the place for you! Not only can you eat traditional Swedish food here, but you can also eat under the goats. That's right—there are live goats grazing on the roof of the restaurant. It all started with Oscar, a birthday goat gag gift from Al's friend Wink Larson.

With a mix of Scandinavian, local, and vegetarian cuisine, you are in for more than you bargained for! Since 1949, Johnson's has been creating memories, down to watching the goats that prance around on the grass roof. Their adjoining Butik features lots of memorabilia including books, jewelry, Swedish linens, housewares, and so much more. It is the perfect place to complement your Door County vacation tour.

Don't even think of leaving this place without tasting the Swedish pancakes. They are wonderful with lingonberries and worth every cent.

10698 N Bay Shore Dr., Sister Bay, 920-854-2626
aljohnsons.com

SAMPLE A BAVARIAN SMORGASBORD
AT THE DORF HAUS

The Dorf Haus Supper Club has been a staple in the Wisconsin food and dining scene since 1959. This second-generation, family-owned restaurant is known for its Bavarian Smorgasbord, which features over 25 homemade items including salads, meats, and desserts.

You will find authentic gems like schnitzel, kartoffle, or even sauerbraten here as you sit and listen to live polka music by the three-piece group Buttons and Banjo as you dine.

As you look around at the antiques, paintings of German castles and kings, and stained glass, you can't help but feel immersed in the culture.

The smorgasbord isn't a daily offering, so mark your calendars; it is served from 5–9 p.m. on the first Monday of each month and the first and third Mondays from June to August.

8931 County Rd. Y, Sauk City, 608-643-3980
dorfhaussupperclub.com

DINE WITH DILLINGER
AT LITTLE BOHEMIA

If you're looking for an interesting dining experience, look no further than Little Bohemia in Manitowish Waters. This restaurant is famous for being the place where John Dillinger and his gang hid out after a robbery in 1934.

Built in 1929, Little Bohemia became a mecca of relaxation for many, including the Chicago criminal element. Dillinger and his gang were no exception. The evidence of the poorly executed FBI raid still remains today as the bullet holes that grace the walls and glass windows are encased for posterity.

Today, the restaurant is a popular spot for tourists and locals alike. The menu features traditional ethnic dishes such as pork shank, sauerkraut, and pork schnitzel. There's also a wide variety of sandwiches, pizzas, pastas, and salads to choose from. You might just get a taste of history as well.

5625 Little Bohemia Ln., Manitowish Waters, 715-543-8800
littlebohemialodge.com

FUN FACT

The film *Public Enemy* was shot in Wisconsin during the summer of 2008. Little Bohemia was one of the locations that they used to tell the story of John Dillinger and his gang.

They did take a little creative license with the ending to create exciting action scenes around their demise.

TRY A BEER FLIGHT
AT MOBCRAFT BREWERY AND TAPROOM

With over 200 microbreweries in Wisconsin, it can be difficult to choose a favorite. The reason people love Mobcraft is their unique business model—they let the people choose what beer they want brewed each month! That's right, you get to vote on the next beer that will be brewed. Talk about customer service! The crowdsourcing makes for a unique twist.

Mobcraft also offers a variety of fun events throughout the year. From Trivia in the Taproom to live music, there's always something going on at Mobcraft. And of course, they offer beer flights, so you can try a little bit of everything!

Maybe you want to try a fruited Witbier like their Get Razzy With It. Or you could try their unique Blue Stone Crush, which is like a smoothie in a glass. All the names are whimsical, like Fish Fry Rye and Kringle Monster. They truly blend the flavors of Wisconsin traditions into their offerings.

505 S 5th St., Milwaukee, 414-488-2019
mobcraftbeer.com

TIP
Get one of their giant pretzels to cleanse your palate between beer samples.

OTHER AMAZING
WISCONSIN MICROBREWERIES

Titletown Brewing
320 N Broadway, Green Bay, 920-437-2337
titletownbrewing.com

The Brewing Projekt
1807 N Oxford Ave., Eau Claire, 715-598-1836
thebrewingprojekt.com

The Lone Girl Brewing Company
114 E Main St., Waunakee, 608-850-7175
thelonegirl.com

Rebellion Brewing
N57 W6172 Portland Rd., Cedarburg, 262-421-8678
rebellionbrewingusa.com

Ooga Brewing
301 Spring St., Beaver Dam, 920-306-5100
oogabrewing.com

H. H. Hinder Brewing Co.
804 Churchill St., Waupaca, 715-942-8018
hinderbrewingco.com

City Service Brewing
404 Main St., Darlington, 608-482-5212
cityservicebrewing.wixsite.com

Central Waters
351 Allen St., Amherst, 715-824-2739
centralwaters.com

CATCH A FRIDAY FISH FRY
AT THE MAPLE TREE

Wisconsin Fish Frys are a longstanding tradition with roots in a strong Catholic population. While there are many places to get your fix of fish, fries, and slaw, not all places are created equal. It doesn't matter if you are sitting in a place that feels like a banquet hall or supper club as long as the drinks are stiff, the food is hot, and the service is great.

The Maple Tree of McFarland has been family owned since 1985 and is the go-to place for great fish. Your Friday dinner includes a choice of potato, full salad and soup bar, and even warm loaves of bread brought right to your table. The Friday offerings include lightly breaded or battered cod and even lake perch. It is the perfect way to start out your weekend, but be prepared for longer wait times during Lent.

6010 US Hwy. 51, McFarland, 608-838-5888
mapletreesupperclub.com

TIP
Get there early on a Friday night to get on the list as they don't take reservations.

OTHER GREAT FISH FRY PLACES

Aunt Mary's Hooterville Inn
10992 Division St., Blue Mounds, 608-437-5444
hootervilleinn.com

Crawfish Junction
W6376 Cty Hwy. A, Johnson Creek, 920-648-3550
crawfishjunction.com

Daddy Maxwell's
150 Elkhorn Rd., Williams Bay, 262-245-5757.
daddymaxwells.com

The Duck Inn
N6214 WI-89, Delavan, 608-883-6988
duckinndelavan.com

Lakefront Brewery
1872 N Commerce St., Milwaukee, 414-372-8800
lakefrontbrewery.com

Owl's Nest
617 E North St., Poynette, 608-635-2298
owlsnestwi.com

Stolley's Hogg Alley
2008 N Venice Beach Rd., Oconomowoc, 262-646-5652
stolleyshoggalley.com

Toby's Supper Club
3717 S Dutch Mill Rd., Madison, 608-222-6913
tobyssupperclub.com

EAT A BUTTERBURGER™
AT CULVER'S

Since 1984, Culver's has been tempting families with their unique twist on the standard hamburger. They are most known for their ButterBurgers, which are fresh (never frozen) beef patties served on a toasted butter bun with your choice of toppings.

The original store is in Sauk City, where Craig and Lea Culver opened it with help from Craig's parents George and Ruth, and it soon exploded into a franchise that not only covers the state of Wisconsin but encompasses more than 850 restaurants over 26 states in the United States.

In addition to burgers, Culver's also offers a variety of chicken dishes, sandwiches, salads, and even frozen custard. And of course, you can't visit Wisconsin without trying their cheese curds!

Culver's has locations all over the state, over 140 of them in fact, so you're never too far from a delicious meal. And bonus points—they're open late! So, whether you're looking for a quick lunch or a late-night snack, Culver's has you covered.

culvers.com

INDULGE IN
A RACINE KRINGLE
AT O&H BAKERY

Racine is known for kringle! The Racine Danish kringle is a flaky, buttery pastry that is filled with fruit or nuts and then hand-rolled into a distinctive shape. It's no wonder that this treat was named the Official State Pastry of Wisconsin in 2013!

There are several kringle bakeries in Racine, but our favorite is O&H Danish Bakery. This family-owned bakery has been making kringles since 1949, and they use the original recipes passed down over generations.

O&H offers a variety of flavors including raspberry, almond, blueberry, and even pumpkin spice. Yes, they have other fun things like donuts and kolache in their pastry cases, but trust me and go for the kringle.

If you can't make it to Racine, don't worry—they ship their kringles all over the country!

4917 Douglas Ave., Racine, 262-637-8895
ohdanishbakery.com

EAT GARBAGE
AT FRANKS DINER IN KENOSHA

If you're looking for a delicious, filling meal, Franks Diner is the place to go! You can't go wrong with any of their menu items, but their garbage plates are especially popular. They are the diner's signature dish.

You start with a half plate with just three eggs or a full plate with five and keep going from there. They are mixed into a combination of hash browns, green peppers, and onions.

- Add your meat or meats (ham, bacon, sausage, chorizo, or Spam) or try their scratch-made corned beef hash.
- Choose from American, cheddar, Swiss, hot pepper jack, feta, or mozzarella to add your cheese.
- Don't eat meat? No problem! There's a veggie option.

The fully loaded garbage plate is also just part of their Red Men Challenge—where you have 45 minutes to eat an insane amount of food. Who doesn't want braggin' rights for eating a lot of garbage?

508 58th St., Kenosha, 262-657-1017
franksdinerkenosha.com

GET A WISCONSIN STATE FAIR
CREAM PUFF

The Wisconsin State Fair is a huge summer tradition for many locals and visitors alike, and while there is a variety of things to see and do, hands-down one of the most popular things to eat is a cream puff.

With 300,000 to 400,000 sold each year, it ranks right up there with watching the racing pigs or flying over the park in the Sky Glider.

These puffs are made fresh daily by a team of 180 people during the 11 days of the fair and are served with a heaping mound of whipped cream and sprinkled with powdered sugar.

If you think one is enough, think again! They are so good that many people come back for seconds . . . or thirds, although each one is large enough to share with a friend.

What is the current price? The current price of a cream puff is $5 with discounts for three-packs and six-packs, and they are only available during that 10-day stretch in August.

Wisconsin State Fair Park
640 S 84th St., West Allis, 414-266-7000
wistatefair.com

RIP INTO
A PAPER BAG PIE
FROM THE ELEGANT FARMER

Since 1991, the good folks at the Elegant Farmer have been making the best apple pie you can wrap your lips around. No applesauce-like pie filling here; their carefully sourced Ida Red apples are lovingly encased in their sugar cookie–like top crusts by hand and then placed inside a paper bag before baking. At a specific time during baking, a hole is cut into the bag to vent that last bit of steam, but not before the apples are perfectly steam-cooked to perfection.

The apple pies are sold (almost half a million each year) in those same bags, and that is why you have to rip into them. But don't take my word for it—grab one for yourself!

1545 Main St., Mukwonago, 262-363-6770
elegantfarmer.com

ENJOY A PASTY
AT THE RED ROOSTER CAFE

A pasty is a hand-held pie typically filled with meat and vegetables. They were originally brought over to the Upper Midwest by Cornish immigrants who worked in the mines, and they quickly became a staple food for miners and their families.

Today, you can find pasties all over Wisconsin, but my favorite place to get one is the Red Rooster in Mineral Point. The Red Rooster has been serving up delicious pasties for over 50 years and through three generations. Their meat pies have a well-seasoned mixture of cubed steak, potato, onion, and rutabaga.

The pasties at the Red Rooster are big enough to be a meal on their own, but you can also get a variety of sides, including coleslaw. They serve it with chili sauce or ketchup, but you can ask for beef gravy. Make sure you save room for some Figgy Hobbin!

They are open seven days a week, but only for breakfast and lunch.

158 High St., Mineral Point, 608-987-9936
facebook.com/lawingersredroostercafe

EAT CHEESE CURDS
FROM THE DANE COUNTY FARMERS MARKET

Dane County Farmers Market is the largest producer-only farmers market in the country. That means that everything you find at the market is made, grown, or raised by the person selling it to you.

The market runs every Saturday from April through November and sells everything from fresh fruits and vegetables to flowers and plants. You can also find meat, baked goods, honey, and the best Wisconsin cheese.

One of the most popular things to buy at the Dane County Farmers Market is fresh cheese curds. Forget the deep-fried version you think you know; real Wisconsinites prefer the fresh, non-breaded, squeaky version of this dairy treat. The toughest choice you will have to make over your cheesy bites of heaven is between white and yellow.

You can find the Dane County Farmers Market on the square in downtown Madison.

TIP

Fresh cheese curds lose their squeak usually within 24 hours. You can get it back by popping them in the microwave for about 15 to 20 seconds.

GET A BOWL OF BOOYAH
AT THE BOOYAH SHED

Booyah is a thick soup made with beef, chicken, or veal with vegetables that is slow-cooked for hours. It's a northeastern Wisconsin tradition that dates back to the 1800s when Belgian and French immigrants settled in the state.

While the exact origins are unclear, everyone can agree that it is delicious, and the best place to get it is at the Booyah Shed.

The Booyah Shed was a food truck in the Green Bay area that specialized in this delicious dish for 10 years. They now have a brick-and-mortar location with a BBQ-joint feel, allowing them to have a much more extensive menu.

Their secret to yumminess? They slow-cook a chicken-only version in a 45-gallon cast-iron kettle. The beans they use are a mix of green and yellow—a subtle nod to the Green Bay Packers and a complement to all the other chunky ingredients.

1800 S Ashland Ave., Green Bay, 920-371-6249
thebooyahshed.com

TIP
Pair it with their Perky Porter Pulled Pork Sandwich for the perfect meal.

SAMPLE A FIRE BOX OLD FASHIONED
AT ROUND MAN

If you're looking for a unique take on a classic Wisconsin cocktail, be sure to stop by Round Man Brewing and try their Fire Box Old Fashioned.

Round Man Brewing is a small, family-owned brewery in downtown Spooner, Wisconsin, that brews several varieties of beer and serves amazing food as well. Instead of the usual micro-brewery pizza and pretzels, you will find everything from poutine to roasted rainbow trout.

Almost as fun to watch being made as it is to drink, their old fashioned is made with Rogue whiskey, demerara syrup, and smoked orange bitters.

They smoke it right before your eyes and then pour it into the perfect glass with one giant ice cube, which keeps it cold without watering it down.

234 Walnut St., Spooner, 715-939-1800
roundmanbrewing.com

TIP
Order the smoked duck nachos to go with it!

SIP AN ICE CREAM DRINK
AT THE BUCKHORN

Since the 1940s, blended alcoholic ice cream drinks have been a staple in Wisconsin supper clubs. Golden Cadillacs, Grasshoppers, and even Pink Squirrels can be seen gracing a table after a nice dinner yet today.

It seems to be a contest for who can pile it the highest. The Buckhorn in Milton, Wisonsin, is no exception. One drink is beyond generous and enough to share with a tablemate.

The Grasshopper seems to be the most popular, but don't be afraid to switch it up with one of the other vintage flavors.

A Pink Squirrel is made of ice cream, crème de noyaux, and white crème de cacao. A Golden Cadillac combines galliano or amaretto, white crème de cocoa, and ice cream.

Whichever you choose to indulge in, you won't be disappointed. Ensure you have a designated driver, as these drinks pack quite the punch!

11802 N Charley Bluff Rd., Milton, 608-868-2653
facebook.com/thebuckhorn

DIP IT
AT CHALET LANDHAUS INN

Wisconsin is a great place to dip into something new, especially if that something is cheese fondue. Since 1985, the folks at Chalet Landhaus Inn have taken this classic dish to new heights with their unique ingredients and atmosphere.

Their cheese fondue is rich, creamy, and delicious, made with all locally produced cheeses, including Roth Kase's famous gruyere cheese. Not a cheese fan? Try their beef fondue, which comes with a pot of bubbling oil, several sauces for dipping, and fresh fruit salad for dessert.

The best part is that each fondue entrée includes their special house salad or cup of homemade soup, fresh-baked rolls, and their famous Rösti potatoes. If you get a chance to try their Swiss onion soup, take it! It is similar to French onion soup but much creamier.

801 State Rd. 69, New Glarus, 608-527-5234
chaletlandhaus.com

TIP
Get the half and half plate with their potatoes and spaetzle if you can.

EAT A SHEBOYGAN BRAT
AT MIESFELD'S

Miesfeld's Market is a family-owned business making bratwurst since 1941. The Sheboygan Brat is a pork sausage usually seasoned with garlic, salt, and pepper, but Miesfeld's has a secret family recipe. It is then grilled, boiled, or baked.

Saturdays are when the magic happens. They host a fundraising hut on their property and a different nonprofit does a brat fry each week. They receive everything (meat, rolls, etc.) from the market at a reduced cost. They then sell the brats and burgers at the retail price and keep the difference. Many organizations will also bring baked goods that are provided by their organization and sell those as well.

It's the perfect way to get a delicious yet thrifty meal and support your community simultaneously!

4811 Venture Dr., Sheboygan, 920-565-6328
miesfelds.com

TIP

Make sure you actually go into Miesfeld's and check out their 25 different flavors of brats.

JUST SIP IT
AT WOLLERSHEIM WINERY

There is something about Wisconsin grapes that makes for a unique wine. It is a cold-hardy gem, perfect for our climate. Wollersheim Winery, located on the Wisconsin River near Prairie du Sac, has tamed them to perfection.

Founded in 1972 on land that had been used for winemaking since the 1840s, it has won countless accolades throughout its history and is now a leader in the Midwest wine business.

Wollersheim offers flight tastings daily and reservable guided walking tours on the weekends. During your visit, you'll be able to sample some of their wines and cocktails, and you may even visit their underground aging caves!

Please note that they do not allow carry-in food or drink, but there's no need to worry; you won't leave this place hungry or thirsty!

Be sure to try their Two Mile Bourbon, matured in fresh, charred American oak barrels after being distilled from their High-Rye recipe mash.

7876 State Rd. 188, Prairie du Sac, 608-643-6515
wollersheim.com

OTHER NOTABLE WISCONSIN WINERIES

Cedar Creek Winery
N70 W6340 Bridge Rd., Cedarburg, 262-377-8020
cedarcreekwinery.com

Dancing Dragonfly Winery
213 120th Ave., Saint Croix Falls, 715-483-9463
dancingdragonflywinery.com

Harbor Ridge Winery
4690 Rainbow Ridge Ct., Egg Harbor, 608-449-4987
harborridgewinery.com

Hawk's Mill Winery
W8170 Pilz Rd., Browntown, 608-966-4295
hawksmillwinery.com

O'Neil Creek Winery
15369 82nd St., Bloomer, 715-568-2341
oneilcreekwinery.com

Villa Bellezza Winery & Vineyard
State Hwy. 35, 1420 3rd St., Pepin, 715-442-2424
villabellezza.com

von Stiehl Winery
115 Navarino St., Algoma, 920-487-5208
vonstiehl.com

Check Out the Little House in the Big Woods (page 47)

MUSIC AND ENTERTAINMENT

GO MEDIEVAL
AT THE BRISTOL RENAISSANCE FAIRE

It's easy to see why the Bristol Renaissance Faire, which features a recreation of the legendary visit of Queen Elizabeth I to the city of Bristol in the year 1574, has been touted as the number-one renaissance faire in the US for 10 years now.

Not far from Kenosha in the town of Bristol, this is a medieval-themed faire that takes place every summer. The faire is held on weekends from late July to early September, and it's a great event for people of all ages.

Attendees can browse the many shops, eat period-appropriate food, watch shows and performances, and even participate in some of the games and activities. There's something for everyone at the Bristol Renaissance Faire and you can even attend in costume!

renfair.com/bristol

WALK THROUGH
THE ROTARY BOTANICAL GARDEN
HOLIDAY LIGHT SHOW

From mid-November to early January, the Rotary Botanical Garden in Janesville is transformed into a winter wonderland with over 1.2 million lights in their themed gardens.

You can smell the oak leaves that have recently fallen, hear the kids cry in delight as they look around through their holographic glasses, and see adorable senior citizen couples smooching while sitting on a bench for a photo. Watch the mini elf house for a bit and see how many kids try to peek inside to see what toys are being made. Enjoy looking at the reflection of the lights off the pond as holiday music plays in the background.

The Holiday Light Show is a great activity for families and is the botanical garden's biggest fundraiser. The best part? If you get cold, you can warm up with a cup of hot chocolate or get a snack.

1455 Palmer Dr., Janesville, 608-752-3855
rotarybotanicalgardens.org

TIP
Sit on one of the many benches available and people watch for a bit. It's the best way to get in the holiday spirit!

SEE A DRIVE-IN MOVIE
AT SKYWAY DRIVE-IN THEATER

Known as the longest-running drive-in theater in Wisconsin, the Skyway is the epitome of traditional outdoor family fun. Inheriting the business from their parents, Jeffrey and Dale Jacobson provide visitors the opportunity to relive their childhood memories of drive-in theaters or give first-time visitors an experience they've never had before.

You will feel like you've stepped back in time when you hit the concession stand and get treats for the movie, with prices like a large popcorn for only six dollars.

The play structures for the kids are a great way for them to burn off energy as they wait for darkness to fall and the movie to start, and you can sit in your own lawn chair to supervise them. They really thought of everything!

3475 State Hwy. 42, Fish Creek, 920-854-9938
doorcountydrivein.com

TIP
If you want to listen to the movie over the radio, save your car battery and bring that old-fashioned boom box with you.

OTHER DRIVE-IN MOVIE THEATERS IN WISCONSIN

Big Sky Drive-In
9174 Winnebago Rd., Wisconsin Dells, 608-254-8025
bigskydrivein.com

Chilton Twilight Drive-In
1255 E Chestnut St., Chilton, 920-849-9565

Field of Scenes Drive-In
N3712 Hwy. 55, Freedom, 920-788-1935

Moonlight Drive-In
1494 E Green Bay St., Shawano, 715-524-3636
shawanocinema.com/#outdoortheater

Sky-Vu Drive-In
1936 State Route 69, Monroe, 608-325-4545
goetzskyvu.com

Stardust
995 22nd St., Chetek, 715-458-4587
stardustdriveinmovie.com

Starlite 14 Drive-In
US Hwy. 14 E, Richland Center, 608-647-3669
facebook.com/starlite14drivein

HANG WITH YOUR PEEPS
AT THE RACINE ART MUSEUM

The Racine Art Museum is a great place to spend an afternoon, especially if you're with your "peeps." Yes, that's right—we're talking about the marshmallow candy.

The Racine Art Museum is home to the annual Peeps art competition, featuring artwork made out of those little marshmallow candies. Every year, artists from all over the country, and occasional entries from outside of the US, submit their Peeps creations in hopes of winning a prize.

The competition is open to both professionals and amateurs, and the 150 to 200 entries are always creative and often hilarious. Even if you're not a fan of Peeps, it's worth checking out the spring exhibit.

In addition to the Peeps art, the Racine Art Museum also has a great collection of contemporary art. So whether you're a fan of Peeps or not, there's something for everyone at the Racine Art Museum.

441 Main St., Racine, 262-638-8300
ramart.org

FEED THE ANIMALS
AT A DRIVE-THROUGH SAFARI

Safari Lake Geneva is a natural wildlife preserve home to animals from around the world. This animal haven is a family-operated business and is considered one of Wisconsin's most exotic by animal expert "Jungle" Jay Christie.

Safari Lake Geneva isn't what most people expect in an animal rescue: the animals are allowed to move around freely while the people who visit are confined to "cages" or cars. This space allows animals to interact with other animals just as they would in their own homes at different locations worldwide.

Animals will come up to you if you have one of the 40-ounce buckets full of a nut-free, corn-based pellet that all the animals you encounter will enjoy. You purchase these at the beginning of your tour or online, and it helps you experience another aspect of this adventure.

W1612 Litchfield Rd., Lake Geneva, 262-582-2094
safarilakegeneva.com

TIP
It is open seasonally, May through October.

PREDICT THE WEATHER
WITH JIMMY THE GROUNDHOG

Sorry Punxsutawney Phil; for over 70 years, Jimmy the Groundhog in Sun Prairie has been more accurate in his predictions. The true prognosticator of prognosticators, Jimmy has his own fan base that braves the Wisconsin cold every year on February 2 to indulge in the whimsy and ceremony of the occasion.

Sun Prairie makes a grand event out of it, with special offers all around the community. You can grab a groundhog latte at Beans n Cream Coffeehouse, buy a groundhog stuffed animal or ornament at Prairie Flowers & Gifts, or even try a groundhog pizza at Sal's (in name only; no real groundhogs are used). Add in the Fun Prairie Frozen Fest activities that cover everything from ice carving to the Hibernation Hustle, and you have a fun family event to check out.

No worries, animal lovers, Jimmy is ethically sourced each year.

Cannery Square, across from City Hall
300 E Main St., Sun Prairie, 608-837-4547
sunprairiechamber.com

TIP
Dress warm—this event is outdoors in early February.

EXPERIENCE
THE HOUSE ON THE ROCK

This bizarre and eccentric house was built by Alex Jordan, Jr. in 1945 and sits atop Deer Shelter Rock. It opened its doors to the public in 1959 and is full of strange and fascinating things that draw your eye from the moment you step inside. From life-sized dolls to vintage cars, there's something for everyone at the House on the Rock.

One favorite is the carousel. It has as many as 269 carousel animals and more than 20,000 lights. The striking feature of the carousel is that there are no horses.

You can expect to experience a replica of an early 20th-century American town, nautical exhibits with a 200-foot sea creature, and a huge collection of automatic music machines. Next, challenge your fear of heights with the Infinity Room. With over 3,000 windows you have an amazing almost 360-degree view of the valley below. How far will you venture out is the only question to ask yourself.

5754 State Rd. 23, Spring Green, 608-935-3639
thehouseontherock.com

TIP
Give yourself several hours to go through this if you really want to see everything.

ESCAPE TO THE MITCHELL PARK DOMES
OF MILWAUKEE

Designed by renowned architect Donald Grieb, the Mitchell Park Domes opened in 1963 to offer an affordable way to see a lot of exotic horticultural gems.

In the three beehive-shaped glasshouses known as the domes, you can experience the desert, the tropics, and whatever seasonal showcase is currently featured. Each dome has its own climate zone showcasing a collection of plants from around the world.

You will see a waterfall, a koi pond, an orchid collection, and even an education station where visitors of all ages can learn more about the plants and environments that they thrive in.

The Domes are open year-round, so no matter when you visit, you'll be able to experience the beauty of nature. It really is Milwaukee's greenhouse masterpiece.

524 S Layton Blvd., Milwaukee, 414-257-5611
mitchellparkdomes.com

TIP
Ask for the current kid's scavenger hunt sheet for even more fun.

PLANT YOURSELF
AT THE FARM WISCONSIN DISCOVERY CENTER

If you're looking for interactive exhibits, educational programming, and a way to learn more about Wisconsin's agricultural heritage, then this is the place for you.

Norval Dvorak was the driving force behind this nonprofit gem that farm families and agritourism funded at Norval Dvorak's urging. It is all about the wonder of Wisconsin agriculture, and their slogan "Where Curiosity Grows," reflects their dedication teaching visitors about the miracle of farming.

There are also programs that educate kids about the importance of family farms. You can learn about where our food comes from and have fun doing it with exhibits for every age and interest—from going to the Land O'Lakes Birthing Barn and seeing the miracle of life to a simulation of crop harvesting. You can enjoy tons of exhibits that showcase the diversity of Wisconsin Agriculture.

7001 Grass Lake Rd., Manitowoc, 920-726-6000
farmwisconsin.org

TIP
Challenge each other on the combine harvester simulator.

RIDE
THE ORIGINAL WISCONSIN DUCKS

These WWII-era amphibious vehicles have six wheels for maximum traction on land and a propeller for water operation. Since 1946, they have been providing land and water tours of the immediate area in the Wisconsin Dells.

With over 90 Ducks, they have the largest collection in the world and are ready to entertain anyone willing to listen with their unique blend of humor and educational insight to the history and geology of the area. The tours are an educational experience for riders of all ages, giving them the opportunity to learn about World War II history while exploring amazing Wisconsin Dells scenery.

Their college student–led tours take visitors around their own wilderness trails in the area overlooking some of the most beautiful scenery in Wisconsin, including the Lower Dells of the Wisconsin River and beautiful Lake Delton. Rest easy— the guides go through a rigorous six-week training program to ensure your safety.

1890 Wisconsin Dells Pkwy., Wisconsin Dells, 608-254-8751
wisconsinducktours.com

CHECK OUT
THE LITTLE HOUSE
IN THE BIG WOODS

Do you have a fan of Laura Ingalls Wilder among you? Then a visit to the Little House in the Big Woods is a must. This gem of a family destination has three parts: the log cabin, the museum, and the gift shop. The museum is the only place that charges a modest fee to visit.

The Pepin community built the log cabin based on the account of Ingalls Wilder from her first book. It sits on the location of her birth and is open to (self) tours year-round.

The cabin sits unfurnished but boasts a fireplace, a loft, two bedrooms, and an information center where you can find out everything you need to know about Laura and her family.

Close by is the Laura Ingalls Wilder Museum. The museum features several replicas of items from the Ingallses's lives as the rooms are transformed to reflect the era they lived in. It is right next to the gift shop.

N3238 Country Rd. CC, Stockholm
lauraingallspepin.com

HUNT THE HODAG
IN RHINELANDER

According to reports from 1893, the Hodag is described as a beast with the head of a frog; the grinning face of a giant elephant; thick, short legs set off by huge claws; the back of a dinosaur; and a long tail with spears at the end.

This seven-foot-long, 30-inch-tall monster has been a Rhinelander legend for over 100 years. If you're lucky, you might spot one while in town, as they have been known to frequent the city streets and even go into local businesses. The Hodag is a great way to get kids involved in learning about the area's history while having fun.

The best place to start your search is at the Visitors Center, where you can pick up a Hodag Hunt passport. Make your way around town and have your passport stamped at each of the 24 locations. When it's full, return it to the Visitors Center for a prize.

Rhinelander Area Chamber of Commerce
450 W Kemp St., Rhinelander, 715-365-7464
explorerhinelander.com/what-is-the-hodag/hodag-finder

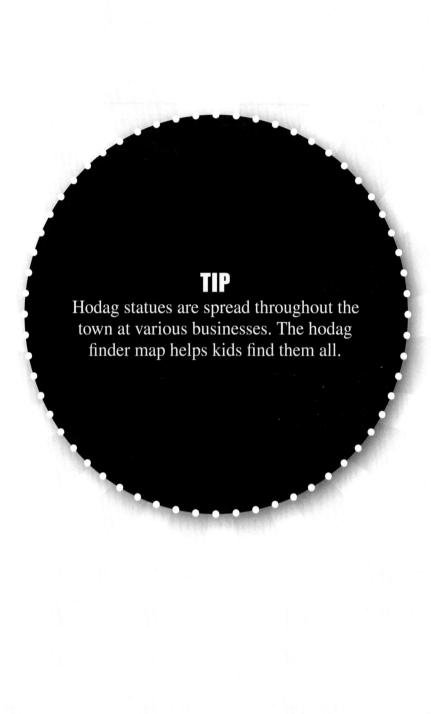

TIP

Hodag statues are spread throughout the town at various businesses. The hodag finder map helps kids find them all.

LEARN THE HISTORY OF SASSAFRAS DRINKS
AT THE MUSEUM OF ROOT BEER

Yes, there is a root beer museum, and it's in Wisconsin! This small but charming museum features the detailed history of sassafras drinks through educational items and a huge collection of root beer memorabilia.

Did you know that sassafras was once used as a medicine? Or that there are over 1,500 different root beer brands in the US? Do you know how some brands rose to the top of the list and became household names?

Learn all of this and more during your visit, and then step up to the counter to either sample from a root beer flight featuring a selection of on-tap offerings, or indulge in a root beer float. You can even select from the multiple different brands on display to assemble a root beer box to take home.

513 Broadway St., Wisconsin Dells, 608-393-8283
museumofrootbeer.com

TIP
Make sure you sit in the back room
and check out all the vintage root beer
commercials. They are a hoot!

TAKE THE CHALLENGE
AT WIZARD QUEST

When a very artistically talented family puts their skills and heads together, they create an amazing series of adventures in a 30,000-square-foot magical place that helps you combine fantasy with team building.

With the help of your tablet, you can choose from many creatures throughout the different realms (fire, water, air, and earth) who need your help. You can decide whether or not to take on a quest; if you do, you will answer a series of interactive questions to find the solution. This really encourages working together, because there is so much to see and remember.

Dress comfortably as you will go up fairy stairs, go down a slide, climb a tree, and more while advancing through your quests. I would suggest you not be the person who crawls under the ogre.

400 Broadway, Wisconsin Dells, 608-253-0324
wizardquest.com

DREAM
AT BOOKWORM GARDENS

Bookworm Gardens is a one-of-a-kind, storybook botanical garden designed to inspire children's love of reading, plants, and nature.

The three-acre-plus gardens feature more than 70 classic kids' books in a variety of different themed areas. There are sculptures and interactive elements throughout the gardens that bring the stories to life with plenty of seating space so you can grab the laminated story pages and just experience it with the littles.

Some of the favorites include *Where the Wild Things Are*, *The Little House in the Big Woods*, and *The Secret Garden.*

The gardens are open seasonally from April through October. They also offer a variety of educational programs for school groups and families. Feel free to pack a picnic lunch—they have tables by The Magic School Bus. Remember to dress for the weather.

1415 Campus Dr., Sheboygan, 920-287-7895
bookwormgardens.org

TIP
Their special events fill up quickly, so keep an eye on their website.

ENJOY AN OUT-OF-THIS-WORLD CELEBRATION
IN ELMWOOD

In the 1970s, dozens of Elmwood residents reported UFO sightings. In a strange coincidence, residents stopped seeing UFOs around the time that UFO Days began in 1977.

Nevertheless, Elmwood's UFO Days is the oldest UFO celebration in Wisconsin. During the final weekend of July, this "UFO capital of Wisconsin" contender goes all-out for a good time.

The celebration is full of small-town activities with a twist. Satisfy your curiosity with a tour of locations where UFO sightings have occurred. Explore your inner artist by painting your own UFO or by trying your luck at Chicken Poop Bingo. Kids are welcome to ride the kiddie train and fire engine.

UFO Days concludes with everyone watching the night sky for spectacular fireworks.

facebook.com/ufodayselmwood

FUN FACT
Elmwood is the longest running UFO festival in Wisconsin, but they also have festivals in Dundee and Belleville.

ROCK OUT
AT MILWAUKEE'S SUMMERFEST

Summerfest, the world's largest music festival, is the place to be each summer. From the end of June through early July, over a thousand concerts are held on 11 stages. This event takes place next to Lake Michigan, making the festival the ultimate summer experience.

Enjoy a wide variety of headlining acts. Past lineups have included Jason Aldean, Lil Wayne, and Lamb of God. Each of Summerfest's various stages offers a unique atmosphere to take in fantastic music performances.

Enjoy music by a variety of entertainers at the Amphitheater, Sausage and Beer Garden, Martini Bar, or Community Park, to name a few.

Families love participating in the Sports Zone's activities or enjoying the lake with the Paddleboat Water Experience. There's also plenty of entertainment, such as kids' workshops for younger children to enjoy.

Henry Maier Festival Park
200 N Harbor Dr., Milwaukee, 414-273-2680
summerfest.com

DISCOVER
DR. EVERMOR'S FOREVERTRON

Take a step into one man's futuristic vision and see the world's largest scrap metal sculpture at Dr. Evermor's Sculpture Park. The park is the home of the Forevertron.

This work of art is constructed entirely from vintage metal. It stands 50 feet tall and over 100 feet wide.

The Forevertron includes lightning rods, Thomas Edison dynamos from the 1800s, power plant components from the 1920s, and even the Apollo 11 spacecraft's decontamination chamber.

The garden includes other metal sculptures as well, and the park and its creator were featured on the show *American Pickers.* This one-of-a-kind attraction should not be missed by anyone who appreciates creativity and dreams of a better future. Make sure to check the website for current hours and information.

S7703 US Hwy. 12, Town of Sumpter, 608-219-7830
worldofdrevermor.com

TIP
It can be challenging to find, but it is behind Delaney's Surplus.

SEE FOLK ART
AT FRED SMITH'S CONCRETE PARK

Walk through a collection of life-size concrete and mixed-media sculptures located at this outdoor museum.

More than 200 sculptures created by "Picasso of the Pines" are housed in the park's collection. Sculptor Fred Smith envisioned characters in the concrete blocks and brought them to life.

There's a story behind each work of art that blends Americana and history. The park features several collective sculptures. "Farming with Horses" is a group of life-size sculptures of farmers with their horses.

Another collective sculpture represents the breaking of a Native American treaty. There are legends represented, such as Paul Bunyan and Ben Hur.

The sculptures have been recognized by *Art in America* magazine. Visit this park to witness uncommon environmental folk art in a common landscape.

N8236 WI-13, Phillips, 715-339-7282
wisconsinconcretepark.org

CATCH A SHOW
AT THE FIRESIDE

The Fireside Theatre opened in 1964 and continues to be operated by the Klopcic family. This unique supper club offers fine dining and live shows with Broadway performers.

The warm atmosphere makes every guest feel welcome and relaxed. This unique supper club is known for its high-quality service and food. The performances here are top-rated.

There are a variety of shows and concerts offered, such as *Grease*, *The Sound of Music*, and even the Midwest comedy *The Church Basement Ladies*.

The Klopcic family values friendliness and quality. It's no surprise that people have continued to return for over 50 years. First-timers and regulars alike rave about the restaurant and entertainment that make the Fireside Theatre such a uniquely enjoyable Midwest experience.

1131 Janesville Ave., Business Hwy. 26 S, Fort Atkinson, 920-477-9505
firesidetheatre.com

TIP
Make sure you arrive a little early to give yourself time to peruse their wonderful gift shops for a souvenir.

Go Spelunking at Cave of the Mounds (page 64)

SPORTS
AND RECREATION

CHEER ON
THE WISCONSIN BADGERS

There are 23 University of Wisconsin sports teams, enough to suit every type of sports fan.

The hockey teams have a long history among the best in the college ranks. A winner of multiple national championships, players from both the men's and women's teams are chosen for Olympic hockey teams. At a Badgers game, it's a joy to watch the hockey players show off their skills and finesse.

The women's volleyball team has won six Big Ten championships. They also won the National Volleyball Championship in 2021. Seeing this accomplished volleyball team is an experience not to be missed.

The football team is one of the 26 college teams that have won more than 900 games. Badgers football fans are more than fans; they are their own culture.

Join in the excitement of game day and experience the legendary "jump around" for yourself.

uwbadgers.com

RIDE THE CAROUSEL
AT THE HENRY VILAS ZOO

The Henry Vilas Zoo in Madison is one of the very few free zoos in the US. This 63-acre lot was gifted to the city in 1904 on the condition that the zoo never charge admission.

In the heart of the children's zoo, you will find the beautiful Conservation Carousel in the carousel building. Since 2006, children of all ages have been able to take a spin on the lovely variety of animals, set to classic carousel music. To ride, you buy tokens on-site for just three dollars each. That money goes toward support of the zoo and its programs.

Of course, there is so much more to do at the zoo! They have educational programming, Keeper Talks, and animals! You can easily spend an entire day here without getting bored—or spending a dime. Pack a picnic and make a day out of it!

702 S Randall Ave., Madison, 608-266-4732
henryvilaszoo.gov

NOTE
The carousel only runs from April through October.

GO SPELUNKING
AT CAVE OF THE MOUNDS

This natural limestone cave near Blue Mounds is one of the coolest year-round adventures you can embark on in Wisconsin.

Formed roughly a million to a million and a half years ago, this family-owned modest show cave will let you experience fascinating geological formations like soda straws, flowstone, lily pads, curtains, oolites, and helictites. Add the blacklight experience to see the calcite formations in all their glory.

Your tour will take you on an adventure that is about a fifth of a mile, over concrete walkways and up and down stairs, traversing about 1,000 of the 1,692 feet of cave.

They maintain the integrity of the cave, protect it, and try to pass its wonders on to their visitors.

Other things you can do there include discovering treasure at the Gemstone Mine, exploring the rock and fossil gift shop, cracking open a geode, hiking the interpretive nature trails, and enjoying the rock and perennial gardens. Some are an additional fee.

2975 Cave of the Mounds Rd., Blue Mounds, 608-437-3038
caveofthemounds.com

TIP
They have a pressed penny machine, so bring two quarters and a shiny new penny.

OTHER WISCONSIN CAVES TO CHECK OUT

Cherney Maribel Caves
in Cherney Maribel Caves County Park of Maribel, WI
maribelcaves.com

Crystal Cave
W965 State Rd. 29, Spring Valley, 715-778-4414
acoolcave.org

Eagle Cave
16320 Cavern Ln., Blue River, 608-537-2988
eaglecave.net

Ledge View Caves
W2348 Short Rd., Chilton, 920-849-1471
ledgeviewnaturecenter.org

St. John Mine
129 S Main St., Potosi

Cave Point
Cave Point County Park, Sturgeon Bay

Kickapoo Indian Caverns
54850 Rhein Hollow Rd., Wauzeka, 608-875-7723
kickapooindiancaverns.com

Apostle Island Sea Caves
La Pointe

Irvine Park Caves
Irvine Park, Chippewa Falls

WALK THROUGH THE TUNNEL
AT LAMBEAU FIELD

Can you call yourself a Green Bay Packers fan if you have never toured Lambeau Field? This is a place all football fans should visit at least once in their lifetime.

The Packers are the only community-owned, nonprofit major league professional sports team in the US. That means that every single shareholder of the team is a Wisconsinite or Wisconsinite wannabe!

Choose between the Classic Stadium Tour, Champion Stadium Tour, and Legendary Stadium Tour as they range from 55 minutes to 120 minutes long and all get you to that tunnel walk onto the field. The longer the tour, the more you see, like the press room or even the visiting team dressing room.

Just picture it now: you're crossing over the historic three bricks and hearing the 80,000-plus fans screaming and cheering as you walk out of the tunnel onto the field . . .

Lambeau Field Stadium Tours
1265 Lombardi Ave., Green Bay, 920-569-7512
packershofandtours.com

OTHER PACKERS-FAN THINGS TO SEE IN GREEN BAY

Packers Heritage Trail
This is a self-guided walking tour that has 25 stops and covers the history of the Packers from their humble beginnings in 1919 as an independent, semipro team to their Super Bowl XLV win. This is free of charge.

Packers Hall of Fame
Located at Lambeau Field, this is a must for every diehard Packers fan. It is a 15,000-square-foot exhibit that chronicles the team's history with interactive displays and artifacts. Tickets are needed for this.

Packers Pro Shop
The official store of the Green Bay Packers is inside Lambeau stadium. Here you can find everything Packer-related, from jerseys to cheesehead hats to tailgating supplies.

Titletown Playground
This is a great place for families with kids as it has 36,000 square feet of football-inspired play space. This is free of charge.

Oneida Walk of Legends
Twenty-four large statues start at Lambeau field and continue east. They cover the legends and the history of the Packers. This is free of charge.

CATCH A PLANE
AT THE EAA MUSEUM

Founded by aviator Paul Poberezny in 1953, the Experimental Aircraft Association (EAA) is now a worldwide organization of aviation enthusiasts.

With a collection to thrill aviation fans of all ages, the EAA Museum is dedicated to preserving the history of aviation.

Its primary purpose is showcasing the homebuilt (kit) aircraft movement, but it also covers vintage and military aircraft. The EAA Museum is a great place to learn about the history of aviation and see some really cool planes up close, as well as to learn about the amazing people who built and flew them.

If you have kids, check out the interactive KidVenture Gallery! They can learn about aerodynamics in fun ways and even try a hang-gliding simulator.

You can also see displays honoring Orville and Wilbur Wright and astronaut Joe Engle of the space program. The EAA Museum has something for everyone.

3000 Poberezny Rd., Oshkosh, 920-426-4818
eaa.org

FUN FACT

One week each year, the EAA AirVenture airshow packs Oshkosh with aviation lovers of all ages. They see a variety of planes, watch incredible air shows, enjoy educational displays, and peruse a huge variety of exhibits.

GET SOAKED
AT THE WISCONSIN DELLS
KALAHARI WATERPARK

You can't go to the Water Park Capital of the World and not dip your toes into the water!

The Kalahari has been a family-owned staple of the Wisconsin Dells since 2000. With both indoor and outdoor water parks, it makes for year-round fun, regardless of the weather.

You can choose to come play at the waterpark for just the day or to stay overnight with waterpark passes included with your room.

Do you want to just play for the day? Make sure to get your tickets online, as they do not always have someone available at the park desk to sell them to you.

With over 750 rooms, it is also a great place to stay if you want to make more than a day out just hitting a water park. Add in their on-site amusement park and multiple restaurants, and it's easy to see why they are so popular.

1305 Kalahari Dr., Wisconsin Dells, 877-525-2427
kalahariresorts.com/wisconsin

TIP
There is no need to take beach towels,
as they have free towels you can check out.

HIKE
THE ICE AGE TRAIL

The Ice Age Trail is a hiking trail that runs for over 1,100 miles through Wisconsin. The trail includes some of the most beautiful and unique landscapes in the state, including glacial lakes, kettles, and moraines that were sculpted by glacial ice over 12,000 years ago.

While you can hike the entire trail, there are also many shorter sections that are perfect for a day hike in the 30 counties it winds through.

From the Door County Peninsula, down through Janesville, back up to the Nicolet National Forest, and then west, the Ice Age Trail has the perfect way for you to explore Wisconsin's unique geology!

One of our favorite sections is the Kettle Moraine State Forest, which includes a variety of trails with different difficulty levels.

No matter what section you choose to hike, you're sure to see some amazing views and maybe even some wildlife.

iceagetrail.org

SPEAR A STURGEON

Lake Winnebago is the only place in the US where you can sturgeon spear. They even created a festival around it! The Sturgeon Spectacular is held in Fond du Lac every year in February, and over the course of three days there are plenty of activities to keep both fishers and non-fishers content.

There are lots of fun Wisconsin Winter activities to choose from, like a downtown hot cocoa and chocolate crawl, snow sculpture competitions, curling, horse-drawn carriage rides, a 5k, and of course, the main event—a competition to spear the largest sturgeon!

Sturgeon can grow up to 15 feet long and weigh over 200 pounds, so this is definitely not your average fishing trip. You might be able to rent a shanty, but you'll need your own decoys, spear, etc.

If you're looking for a unique Wisconsin outdoor experience, this is definitely something you need to add to your list!

sturgeonspectacular.com

SEE
THE BREW CREW

Watching a Brewers game at the American Family Field stadium has been a tradition since they came to town in 1970. People love the friendly atmosphere, the racing sausage mascots, and the spacious, easy-to-navigate stadium.

The stadium itself is worth the visit, with a retractable roof that keeps things comfortable come rain or shine.

You'll have a fantastic time with fellow Brewer fans, whether you're taking part in legendary Wisconsin tailgating, or sitting in the stadium during the game enjoying brats and brews.

See the infamous mascot, Bernie Brewer, help rally the cheering for the home team and then go down the slide into "home plate" when one of the Brewers hits a home run.

The Brew Crew's "Baseball, Beer, and Brats" is an authentic and fun Wisconsin tradition that should be sampled by everyone at least once in their lifetime.

1 Brewers Way, Milwaukee
mlb.com/brewers

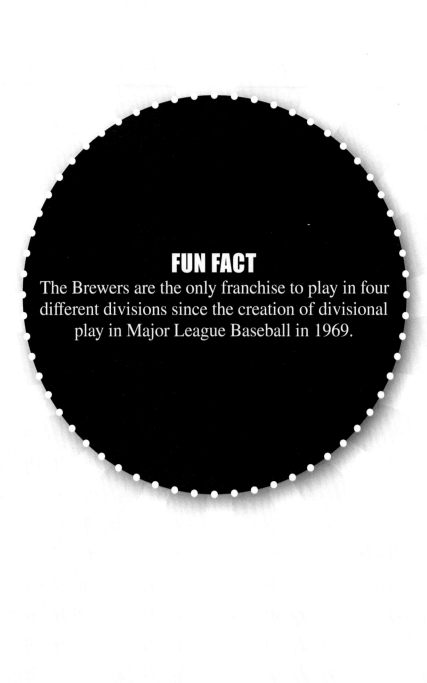

FUN FACT

The Brewers are the only franchise to play in four different divisions since the creation of divisional play in Major League Baseball in 1969.

CATCH THE CHECKERED FLAG
AT ROAD AMERICA

If you're a fan of auto racing, then Road America is a must-visit. This world-famous racetrack is located in the beautiful town of Elkhart Lake, and it hosts a variety of races throughout the year.

Whether you want to watch the pros race or take your own car out on the track with their Sunset Cruising program, Road America has something for everyone. They even offer driving lessons so you can learn from the best with your car or motorcycle.

If you need a break from all the racing, there are plenty of other things to do there through their Group Adventure program, including karting and an off-road experience with Yamaha UTVs. They give you basic instructions and access to tracks and trails.

Not into hands-on activities? Take one of their tours and learn more about America's National Park of Speed.

N7390 State Hwy. 67, Plymouth, 800-365-7223
roadamerica.com

TIP

Most Adventure programs require a minimum of four people 16 and over, with the Racing Adventure requiring you to be 18 and over.

KAYAK
AT CAVE POINT PARK

Cave Point County Park is one of the most popular places to visit in Door County. The park is known for its breathtaking views, crystal clear water, and limestone cliffs.

One of the best ways to experience the beauty of Cave Point is from a kayak! You can rent kayaks from several companies in Door County, or you can bring your own.

Keep a few things in mind if you're planning on kayaking at Cave Point County Park. First, the water is cold—even in summer!—so make sure you dress accordingly. Second, the waves can get pretty big, so it's important to know your skill level and the conditions.

Once you're out on the water, keep your eyes peeled for wildlife.

Finally, don't forget to take plenty of pictures! Cave Point Park is one of the most scenic places in Wisconsin, and you're sure to want to remember your time there.

5360 Schauer Rd., Sturgeon Bay, 920-743-5511
co.door.wi.gov/554/cave-point-county-park

PLACES TO RENT KAYAKS IN THE AREA

Bay Shore Outfitters
59 N Madison Ave., Sturgeon Bay, 920-818-0413
bayshoreoutfitters.com

Cave Point Paddle and Peddle*
6329 WI-57, Jacksonport, 920-868-1400
cavepointpp.com

Door County Adventure Center
4497 Ploor Rd., Sturgeon Bay, 920-746-9999
dcadventurecenter.com

Island Adventure Company
164 Green Bay Rd., Washington Island, 920-421-4563
islandadventurecompany.com

Lakeshore Adventures*
8113 Hwy. 57, Baileys Harbor, 920-839-2055
lakeshore-adventures.com

Peninsula Kayak Company*
6300 Hwy. 57, Jacksonport, 920-918-4314
peninsulakayakcompany.com

*Also gives guided kayak tours in the area

GO RAFTING
ON THE WOLF RIVER

Experience a wilderness adventure complete with sightings that can include black bears, otters, and wolves. This rafting trip gives you the opportunity to tumble down a series of whitewater rapids for the adventure of a lifetime.

The Wolf River has three waterfalls that are over five feet high and several rapids along a route interspersed with calm waters and pools. In between the rapids, take in the beautiful scenery of the wild shoreline.

There are several guides that offer whitewater rafting trips on the Wolf River. There are rafting trips for all skill levels, from beginners to advanced. All rafting trips take place during the day and range from two to six hours. Take your water rafting trip in the summer when the water is warmer and calmer.

wolfriverrafting.com

TIP
Soft sided coolers make things a lot more fun and allow for you to bring drinks and snacks along for your time on the water.

Admire the Woodwork at the Paine Art Center (page 122)

HARLEY-

Have Fun in '51!

Business was good in the years immediately following WWII. As formerly scarce products started to reappear on the market, consumers with money to spend eagerly snapped them up. Harley-Davidson dealers began selling both motorcycles and accessories in record numbers.

"Get in on the good times now!" encouraged the 1951 Harley-Davidson ad campaign, showing young people enjoying the company's new lightweight motorcycles. At the same time, company leaders prepared dealers for difficult times ahead. The days of just sitting around and taking orders are ordinarily gone. We've got to get sales going by creating a demand for our products, Harley-Davidson emerged from WWII prepared to take advantage of postwar opportunities, but the 1950s would present a new set of challenges.

1951

"25"*Superiority*
E SWEEPING
ENDERS

"125"*Beauty*
FIVE FLASHY
COLORS

Learn at the National Historic Cheesemaking Center (page 137)

Dream at Bookworm Gardens (page 53)

Walk through the Tunnel at Lambeau Field (page 66)

Patchouli
andalwood

Sandalwood

Ch

SANDALWOOD
♥ Goat Milk Soap ♥

SANDALWOOD
♥ Goat Milk Soap ▼

ndalwood
Soap ▼

SAN
♥ Go

Dog Shampoo
With essential oils
fleas and ticks dislike

Apple & Pine

Dog Shampoo Bar

♥
Goat
Milk
Soap
♥

Dog Sha

Bar

♥
Goat
Milk
Soap

Get Your Goat Milk Product Fix at Floppy Ear Farm (page 151)

Learn the History of Sassafras Drinks at the Museum of Root Beer (page 50)

Get Your Frank Lloyd Wright Fix at Taliesin (page 120)

Eat Farm-to-Fork
at Salvatore's Tomato Pies (page 8)

Feed the Animals at a Drive-Through Safari (page 41)

Step Back in Time at Heritage Hill (page 118)

Kayak at Cave Point Park (page 78)

CLIMB HOLY HILL

The Basilica of the National Shrine of Mary, Help of Christians is located at the highest point in southeastern Wisconsin. The breathtaking views from the Scenic Tower make this the perfect fall bucket-list item.

Not only will you see all the colors of the changing leaves in the treetops, but it's the perfect day trip for spiritual reflection before the onset of winter.

There is also an arts and crafts fair here in mid-September with over 200 artists and craftsmen set up along the grounds of the basilica.

Explore the stations of the Outdoor Way of the Cross and climb the bell tower. View a rare statue of Mary in the shrine's chapel or attend a Mass here. While you are here, stop by the café to get a coffee or sandwich for lunch.

1525 Carmel Rd., Hubertus, 262-628-1838
holyhill.com

TIP
Make sure you take your camera to catch stunning fall scenes.

CAMP
AT DEVIL'S LAKE STATE PARK

Being the largest state park in Wisconsin, and on the western edge of where the last glacier stopped, Devil's Lake is a popular camping destination for many reasons!

From Effigy Mounds to hiking trails, Devil's Lake has so much to offer anyone who simply wants to connect with nature.

To start with, there are three campgrounds with a total of 423 sites, so there is plenty of room for everyone. The park follows the state online registration system, so you need to reserve your spot in advance—and book early as it fills fast!

The lake is motor free—but feel free to bring that paddle board, canoe, or kayak. The area is known as a very picturesque location for hiking and rock climbing.

There are 30 miles of trails that will take you through some amazing terrain—and if you're lucky, you might even spot some Devil's Lake wildlife!

S5975 Park Rd., Baraboo, 608-356-8301
dnr.wisconsin.gov/topic/parks/devilslake

TIP
There are rattlesnakes in the area, so be mindful when hiking.

OTHER GREAT WISCONSIN STATE PARKS FOR CAMPING

Copper Falls State Park
36764 Copper Falls Rd., Mellen, 715-274-5123
dnr.wisconsin.gov/topic/parks/copperfalls

High Cliff State Park
N7630 State Park Rd., Sherwood, 920-989-1106
wisconsin.gov/topic/parks/highcliff

Kohler Andrae State Park
1020 Beach Park Ln., Sheboygan, 920-451-4080
wisconsin.gov/topic/parks/kohlerandrae

Peninsula State Park
9462 Shore Rd., Fish Creek, 920-868-3258
wisconsin.gov/topic/parks/peninsula

Perrot State Park
W26247 Sullivan Rd., Trempealeau, 608-534-6409
dnr.wisconsin.gov/topic/parks/perrot

Wyalusing State Park
13081 State Park Ln., Bagley, 608-996-2261
dnr.wisconsin.gov/topic/parks/wyalusing

LET IT ROLL
AT THE HOLLER HOUSE

The Holler House is the oldest sanctioned bowling alley in the US. For over 100 years, people have been enjoying this family-owned and operated gem hidden away in the basement of the Holler House Bar.

Step back in time as you walk through the bar, go down the stairs, and see the two-laned, real wood, vintage alley. Pins are reset manually with a "pin-setter" and bowlers keep their own score on paper.

You have to make a reservation to bowl, as pinsetters aren't on duty all the time—and yes, they do have a bowling league!

Get your reservations in early as people come from all over the world to experience this place. Signing up online is easy on their website.

While you are sitting in the bar having a drink and waiting for your turn to bowl, make sure you ask about the 1,000 plus bras hanging from the ceiling!

2042 W Lincoln Ave., Milwaukee, 414-647-9284
geneandmarcyhollerhouse.com

LEARN ABOUT CRANES
AT THE INTERNATIONAL CRANE FOUNDATION

Founded in 1973, the International Crane Foundation (ICF) is a crane conservation organization that works to protect cranes and their wetland habitats around the world.

When you visit the beautiful, 250-acre property, you can expect to see live crane exhibits with 15 different species of cranes. It is the only place in the world where this is possible!

There is also a visitor center, breeding facilities, a research library, and nature trails.

ICF has worked to reintroduce several crane species back into the wild, including the whooping crane in North America and the red-crowned crane in China.

The foundation's work isn't limited to cranes, however. ICF also works to protect other wetland birds, such as waterfowl, shorebirds, and gulls. If you're interested in helping to conserve wetland habitats, be sure to check out the International Crane Foundation. It's a great place to learn about these amazing birds and what we can do to help them.

E11376 Shady Lane Rd., Baraboo, 608-356-9462
savingcranes.org

FOLLOW THE BUCKS

2021 was a big year for both the Milwaukee Bucks and their fans as they won their first championship in over 50 years.

It certainly helps that the "Greek Freak" is considered one of the best basketball players on the planet right now—Giannis Antetokounmpo is a two-time MVP and the magic weapon added to an already incredible team.

The Fiserv Forum is their home, the first bird-friendly stadium in the world. Opened in 2018, this is so much more than a stadium where games are played; they've created an experience that the entire family can enjoy! Take in the Hoop Troop, Bucks Dancers, Mascot Bango, and Bucks Beats Drumline all while cheering on the team.

No standard stadium food here! Try treats from local places like Gold Rush Chicken and Sobelman's.

1111 N Vel Phillips Ave., Milwaukee, 414-227-0500
promotions@bucks.com

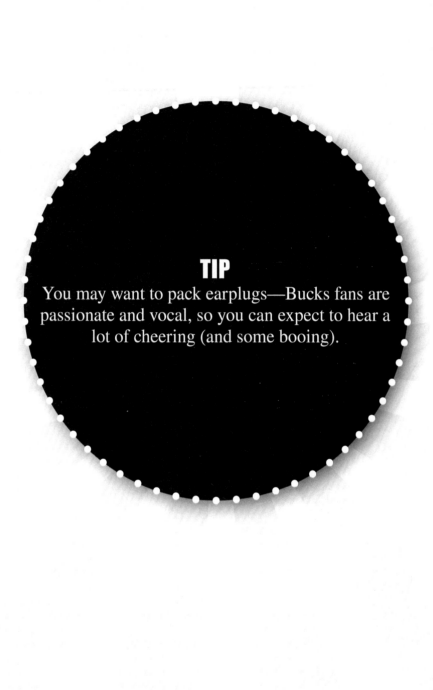

TIP
You may want to pack earplugs—Bucks fans are passionate and vocal, so you can expect to hear a lot of cheering (and some booing).

THROW COW POOP
IN PRAIRIE DU SAC

Step up to the challenge on Labor Day weekend and test your Wisconsinite mettle by entering the Wisconsin Cow Chip Throw.

Both children and adults can compete to be a winning chip chucker, and each contestant gets two chips to test their skill with only the farthest flung being counted.

Have no fear, these hardened, disc-shaped pieces of cow doo are relatively odor-free and easy to handle; they're often referred to as the "nuggets of nastiness."

After getting your hands a little dirty, clean up and take your time to enjoy the rest of the event. Have a bite to eat from several of the food vendors and enjoy the live entertainment.

There's plenty for kids to do besides chucking chips. Family entertainment includes the children's area, which has everything from bounce houses to bumper trucks.

Marion Park, 145 1st St., Prairie du Sac, 608-963-5280
wiscowchip.com

FUN FACT
In 1989, the Wisconsin State Legislature proclaimed the cow chip the Unofficial State Muffin.

GET STARRY EYED
AT THE YERKES OBSERVATORY

Modern astrophysics was born at Yerkes Observatory, which is nestled in a 50-acre landscape. The first pictures of the Andromeda galaxy were captured with a telescope from this observatory around 1900.

The shape of the Milky Way was also discovered here. The Yerkes Observatory is in Williams Bay, on the shores of Geneva Lake. The observatory is made up of historically important telescopes in a beautiful building.

Astronomers Carl Sagan and Edwin Hubble (of the Hubble telescope) were both employed here, and notable scientists such as Albert Einstein visited.

While the Great Refractor telescope is not a modern telescope, it is still an amazing way to view the stars. Step back into an important time of American ingenuity with a tour of this remarkable place of scientific discovery.

373 W Geneva St., Williams Bay
yerkesobservatory.org

TIP
Tours are geared towards those 10 or older.

CHANNEL ELSA
AT EAGLE RIVER'S ICE CASTLE

If you're ever in Wisconsin in the winter and feel like channeling your inner Elsa, you're in luck!

At Eagle River, you'll find an enormous ice sculpture that firefighters and other volunteers build. Using 2,000 massive pieces of ice, they create a beautiful palace perfect for exploring.

Don't worry about getting cold—the fire department has you covered. They've been building these ice palaces for years and have the whole process down to a science.

This takes longer to build than you may think! It tends to draw crowds of people who love to watch the magic happening behind the scenes since the time it takes to make is actually longer than the time each castle is around for viewing.

Once finished, firefighters and volunteers light the tower to memorialize the dead. In 2022, the department decorated the castle in purple in honor of 10-year-old Berklee Adamovich, who passed away from cancer two weeks before Christmas.

116 S Railroad St., Eagle River, 800-359-6315
eagleriver.org/about/ice-castle

TIP
Keep an eye on their website for when they start building it. It is fun to watch the volunteers using the old equipment to make the magic happen.

BUNDLE UP
FOR THE WORLD
SNOWMOBILE HEADQUARTERS

In 1983, a group of friends obsessed with snowmobiles convened in Minocqua to tackle a problem: there was no central headquarters for all things snowmobiles.

The following year, the World Snowmobile Headquarters was established in a one-story structure next to the Eagle River Derby Track in northern Wisconsin.

This place is recognized as the Snowmobile Capital of the World® and has been home to the World Championship Snowmobile Derby for more than 59 years. It's an all-encompassing resource for snowmobiles, and awards honoring the winter sport are on display all around the structure.

The museum is also home to a wide variety of snowmobiles from different eras, making it the perfect place to learn about the history of this fascinating winter sport.

Check out their "Ride with the Champs" winter event, when riders from all over the Midwest come to show off their skills and interact with spectators.

1521 N Railroad St., Eagle River, 715-479-2186
worldsnowmobilehq.com

Learn about the Wisconsin State Capitol Building (page 110)

CULTURE
AND HISTORY

LEARN ABOUT
THE WISCONSIN STATE
CAPITOL BUILDING

Completed in 1917, the State Capitol is one of the most iconic buildings in the state. The building itself is beautiful, but there's also a lot to see inside.

You can take a tour of the Capitol, which is free and open to the public, that takes you through the different floors of the building and highlights some of the most important features, like the only granite dome in the US.

It has different kinds of beautiful marble from all over the world, and the stained glass is stunning, but pay attention to the Edwin Blashfield mural "Resources of Wisconsin" that graces the rotunda ceiling.

The Capitol is also home to several sculptures and paintings, many of which are by Wisconsin artists.

This is a great place to start if you're interested in learning more about Wisconsin history and government, or if you just want to enjoy the only State Capitol to be built on an Isthmus.

2 E Main St., Madison, 608-266-0382
legis.wisconsin.gov/about/visit

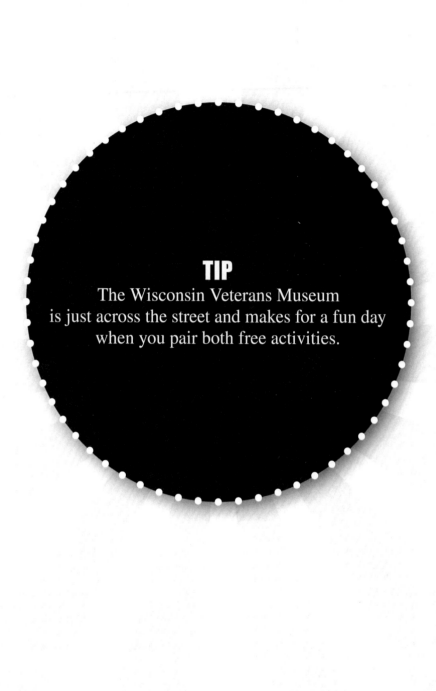

TIP
The Wisconsin Veterans Museum
is just across the street and makes for a fun day
when you pair both free activities.

STEP BACK IN HISTORY
AT OLD WORLD WISCONSIN

Old World Wisconsin is an outdoor living history museum depicting Wisconsin farmsteads from the mid-19th to early 20th centuries. It is one of the largest museums of its kind in the US.

With over 60 historic structures and 25 authentic ethnic farmsteads, it gives you a chance to take a step back in time and experience what life was like over 100 years ago.

This is a great place to take the family as there are things for everyone to do. With 70 historic buildings that have been moved from their original locations and reassembled, you can tour a real one-room schoolhouse, a blacksmith shop, a church, a log cabin, and more. The newest addition? A brewhouse!

They also have many events throughout the year, such as their Harvest Fest or their Christmas in the Country. They also offer a chance to participate in some hands-on workshops like bread baking or quilting.

W372 S9727 Hwy. 67, Eagle, 262-594-6301
oldworldwisconsin.wisconsinhistory.org

TIP
Wear your walking shoes; you can get to different areas of the place faster by walking instead of waiting for the shuttles.

GO HOG WILD
AT THE HARLEY-DAVIDSON MUSEUM

This is a must for any Harley lover or anyone who wants to learn about the rich history of this Wisconsin-based company.

Founded in 1903, Harley-Davidson is one of America's most iconic brands. The museum tells the story of the company, its motorcycles, and the people who have ridden them throughout its more than 100-year history.

More than 450 motorcycles and artifacts are on display, as well as a café, gift shop, and event space. The museum is also home to the world's largest collection of Harley-Davidson motorcycles, with more than 500 on display. What makes their display unique is that they pulled many right off the assembly line directly to their facility for display.

You will also be amazed at the collection of materials used to support the dealership franchises over the years, as well as their involvement in the war efforts.

400 W Canal St., Milwaukee, 877-436-8738
h-dmuseum.com

TIP
Time your visit to eat at the MOTOR® Bar & Restaurant. It is the only Harley-Davidson restaurant.

RIDE
THE MARK TWAIN ZEPHYR

The Wisconsin Great Northern Railroad is home to the World Famous 1935 Art Deco Streamliner called the *Mark Twain* and is the only place in the world where you can ride a Zephyr.

After a long restoration process, this gem that was originally named after the famous author can now be ridden again. All the cars were named after the characters in Twain's books by the CB&Q Railroad in 1935 and have been brought back to life: Injun Joe, Becky Thatcher, Huckleberry Finn, and Tom Sawyer. You will also see the Effie Dean car from the Pioneer Zephyr. (The rest of the Pioneer Zephyr is on display at the Museum of Science and Industry in Chicago.)

Why were the Zephyr trains so fantastic? They had many "firsts," including the first to be made of stainless steel, the first to have a diesel-electric system that was more efficient, and they could go faster than any other train at 122 mph.

N6639 Dilly Lake Rd., Trego, 715-635-3200
spoonertrainride.com

OTHER PLACES FOR TRAIN LOVERS IN WISCONSIN

Mid-Continent Railway Museum
E8948 Diamond Hill Rd., North Freedom, 608-522-4261
midcontinent.org

National Railroad Museum
2285 S Broadway, Green Bay, 920-437-7623
nationalrrmuseum.org

The East Troy Electric Railroad
2002 Church St., East Troy, 262-642-3263
easttroyrr.org

Camp Five Museum & Lumberjack Steam Train
5068 US Hwy. 8 32, Laona, 715-674-3414
lumberjacksteamtrain.com

Mining Museum & Rollo Jamison Museums
405 E Main St., Platteville, 608-348-3301
mining.jamison.museum

Riverside & Great Northern Railway
N115 CR-N, Wisconsin Dells, 608-254-6367
dellstrain.com

CLOWN AROUND
AT CIRCUS WORLD MUSEUM

If you have ever wanted to know more about the Ringling Brothers Circus or the history of the circus in America, Circus World in Baraboo is the place for you. This museum has one of the largest collections of circus wagons in the world, and you can even get a guided tour through them.

It is more than just a circus museum; they keep the traditions alive with a Big Top show that features everything from animal acts to clowns. Watch the interaction between handlers and the elephants, donkeys, and dogs as you are also entertained with trapeze acts and unicycles.

Kids are engaged with a special children's show where participants don't know if they are part of the act or part of the crowd until showtime.

After the shows, take a tour of some of the historic buildings and see how things have changed over the years—or try a ride on an elephant.

550 Water St., Baraboo, 608-356-2884
circusworldbaraboo.org

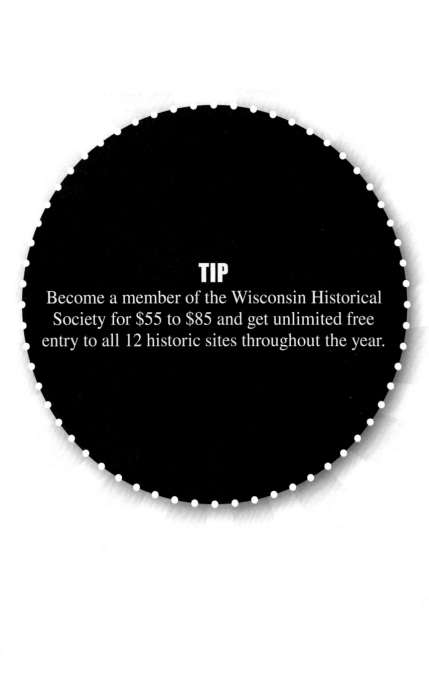

TIP
Become a member of the Wisconsin Historical Society for $55 to $85 and get unlimited free entry to all 12 historic sites throughout the year.

STEP BACK IN TIME
AT HERITAGE HILL

Open air living history museums are a fun way to learn about the history of an area, and Heritage Hill fits the bill perfectly. This is a great place to learn about the early settlers of Wisconsin and how they lived.

With over 40 historic buildings spread over 54 acres, you can tour the homes, churches, and businesses of yesteryear to get a feel for what life was like in the early days of Wisconsin. Add in over 9,000 artifacts that date back to the 17th century and you have a recipe for an educational and entertaining day out.

From Wisconsin's fur-trading days to the establishment of forts like Fort Howard, to the immigration wave that brought a huge variety of agricultural concepts to the state, Heritage Hill has a designated area to teach visitors more.

Make sure you go early enough to watch the soldier raise the American flag at the fort—the attention to detail is amazing.

2640 S Webster Ave., Green Bay, 920-448-5150
heritagehillgb.org

LEARN HISTORY
AT THE KENOSHA CIVIL WAR MUSEUM

No, there was never a Civil War battle in Wisconsin, but this museum in Kenosha does more than just chronicle the events leading up to the Civil War; the museum provides a detailed account of the war itself.

You will learn about the role that Wisconsin played in the conflict, as well as those of some of her fellow upper-Midwest states. We provided a significant number of both men and supplies to the Union army. Over 90,000 Wisconsin men would leave their home for the cause. Kenosha was a major hub for war production, and many of the city's factories were involved in supplying the troops.

Make sure you watch the 10-minute-long film *Seeing the Elephant*. It's shown in a unique 360-degree format and covers the first battle experiences of three different soldiers.

Soldiers, spouses, nurses, children, slaves, and more help to tell this story.

5400 1st Ave., Kenosha, 262-653-4141
museums.kenosha.org/civilwar

GET YOUR FRANK LLOYD WRIGHT FIX
AT TALIESIN

Taliesin is the former home of legendary American architect Frank Lloyd Wright, which spans 37,000 square feet.

Designed and built by Wright himself, it served as his primary residence from 1911 until his death in 1959. It was then bequeathed to the Frank Lloyd Wright Foundation, which continues to operate as a museum and educational center.

At this National Historic Landmark and UNESCO World Heritage Site, a tour will teach you about much more than just his architectural philosophy and family life.

As you walk through Taliesin, you can feel Wright's desire to be in harmony with nature. You will learn how he created his paid apprentice program that would become legendary. You can get a feel for what inspired his designs at the different stages of his life.

All that and more comes to life as you walk through what was literally his workshop and "test kitchen" of ideas.

5607 County Rd. C, Spring Green, 608-588-7900
taliesinpreservation.org

SLEEP ON A SUB
AT THE WISCONSIN MARITIME MUSEUM

The Wisconsin Maritime Museum is one of the unique museums in the state and is also home to one of the state's trendiest Airbnbs.

The USS *Cobia* is a WWII submarine thoroughly repaired and upgraded with modern conveniences. It's ideal for a private Airbnb experience at just $500 for a night! This covers five guests—but you can bring more at just $50 each. Keep in mind the *Cobia* has up to 65 beds! The sub's Airbnb includes bedding and toiletries, light breakfast, coffee, and juice.

As the *Cobia* is part of the active museum, all overnight guests are to be out before 9 a.m. so they can let museum guests and sub tours through. That's why you can only book one night at a time.

There is also an overnight program for youth groups that is very different. Either way, you'll get an experience as unique as the vessel.

75 Maritime Dr., Manitowoc, 920-684-0218
wisconsinmaritime.org

ADMIRE THE WOODWORK
AT THE PAINE ART CENTER

This is a must-see for anyone visiting Oshkosh. The historic mansion is filled with beautiful woodwork, stained glass, and tapestries, along with incredible art.

Built by lumber baron Nathan Paine (who never got to live in it), the home was designed to have both a private residence and a public gallery for showcasing art to the public. Construction was started in 1927, but the completion of this Tudor Revival–style mansion was hampered by not only the Great Depression but also World War II.

As Nathan died in 1947, his wife Jessie chose to open the entire place to the public and fill it with art in 1948 instead of making it her home. This fulfilled the couple's desire to bring both art and culture to Oshkosh.

Each room is more beautiful than the last, and the details carved into the wood are just as stunning as the art collection the building houses.

1410 Algoma Blvd., Oshkosh, 920-235-6903
thepaine.org

TIP

The gardens are also gorgeous.
Make sure you sit by the fountain
for a few minutes and take it all in.

LEARN
AT AMERICA'S BLACK
HOLOCAUST MUSEUM

Founded by the only known survivor of a lynching, the ABHM is the first and only museum of its kind in the US. The experiences of Dr. James Herbert Cameron, Jr. led him to collect over 12,000 artifacts, which he used to tell the stories of Black people in America.

The museum is set up so you go through the exhibits in chronological order, starting with what pre–slave trade African life was like and going on through the centuries, concluding with President Obama. You learn about so much: the brutality and oppression of slavery, the Underground Railroad, what early "freedom" was like, Jim Crow laws, racism, lynching, politics, red-lining, poverty, Juneteenth, hope, and so much more that I simply cannot put it all into words.

Simply put, the museum's mission is to preserve, research, educate, and commemorate the history of African Americans so that we can all be better going forward. It gives a name to the nameless who have been erased from history.

401 W North Ave., Milwaukee, 414-209-3640
abhmuseum.org

CHECK OUT THE UNDERGROUND RAILROAD
AT THE MILTON HOUSE

The Milton House Museum is a must-see for anyone interested in Wisconsin history or the Underground Railroad. You will learn all about the Goodrich family and how they founded Milton, built the community, helped start Milton College, and helped freedom-seekers on their journey based on their Seventh Day Baptist religion.

Built in 1844, it is the last certified Underground Railroad station in Wisconsin that can be toured. Over its life, it has been a stagecoach stop, a train stop, a general store, and even a boarding house.

The museum offers tours led by knowledgeable guides who will tell you all about the history of the house and the people who helped slaves escape to freedom. They even take you through the tunnel where former slaves hid.

Make sure you check out their Civil War Living History Days, held the weekend before Memorial Day weekend!

18 S Janesville St., Milton, 608-868-7772
miltonhouse.org

DIG UP CORNISH HISTORY
AT PENDARVIS

Pendarvis is a restored Cornish mining settlement in Mineral Point, Wisconsin. The settlement was founded in 1827 by Welsh and Cornish immigrants attracted to the area by the lead mines.

Today it is a National Historic Landmark where visitors can tour the restored buildings and learn about both the area's history and the two men responsible for preserving all of that history.

From female Native American miners to the Cornish miner influx, you learn about the journey to build the area, how the miners dealt with the Great Depression, and how they took off to California. You will also learn why Wisconsin is called the "Badger State" from the incredibly informative tour guides.

It is amazing what partners Bob Neal and Edgar Hellum were able to accomplish in a time before most communities were thinking of historic preservation. They started saving their local history in 1935, when it wasn't popular until the mid 1960s.

114 Shakerag St., Mineral Point, 608-987-2122
pendarvis.wisconsinhistory.org

TIP
These are vintage buildings you tour and are not ADA compliant. There are stairs and there is no wheelchair access.

EXPERIENCE LUXURY
AT VILLA LOUIS

If you want to experience Victorian life during the 19th century, then you must visit the estate of one of Wisconsin's most prosperous families. Villa Louis was the country home for the famous Dousman Family, and this estate sits pretty on the banks of the Mississippi River.

The home has been fully restored to the splendor of an era long ago, when life was simpler. You'll be amazed at all that remains from this time period, including original family furnishings!

When you walk through the doors of this magnificent mansion, your imagination becomes transported to a time when wealth and power defined what life was all about.

You even get a peek into what life was like for the servants—their literally different world in the background.

Make sure you take a sip or two from the artesian wells, which are still safe to drink from!

521 Villa Louis Rd., Prairie du Chien, 608-326-2721
villalouis.wisconsinhistory.org

GO THROUGH
BECKMAN MILL

Built in 1868, the historic Beckman Mill is nestled in a valley between two rivers in a 50-acre county park, six miles west of Beloit.

There is a lot to see at the mill complex. They fully restored the mill in 1997, so you can watch as corn is ground using the mill's original water-driven Leffel turbine on the first Saturday of each month.

A tour will teach you the history of the area from the 1830s on as you check out the casks and barrel-making area, blacksmith shop display, creamery display, vintage garden, and more in the park. The park, named after the mill as Beckman Mill County Park, is a nice place to have a picnic, go fishing, or even go hiking after you visit the historic site.

Plan your visit: the mill is only open on Saturdays and Sundays from 1 to 4 p.m., May through October, and a tour costs three dollars per person.

11600 S County Rd. H, Beloit, 608-751-1551
beckmanmill.org

CLIMB
WIND POINT LIGHTHOUSE

As one of Wisconsin's most iconic landmarks, this 108-foot-tall structure has been a beacon for ships since 1880 and has a live-in caretaker to this day.

Now on the National Register of Historic Places, the lighthouse is open to the public for tours and features a museum and gift shop. The best part is that you can climb to the top of the lighthouse! For just $10, you can get this once-in-a-lifetime experience on the first Sunday of each month.

If those dates don't work for you, there is the option to have a private tour. All group members must live within the same household and there is a $60 minimum charge.

Visits to the grounds are always free, 365 days a year, so you can come to swim, picnic, or walk through the beautiful gardens.

After touring the lighthouse and area, make sure to purchase a personalized brick to be placed in the Memorial Brick Garden.

4725 Lighthouse Dr., Racine, 262-639-3777
windpointlighthouse.org

OTHER WISCONSIN LIGHTHOUSES TO CHECK OUT

Cana Island Light Station
8800 E Cana Island Rd., Baileys Harbor, 920-743-5958
dcmm.org/cana-island-lighthouse

Eagle Bluff Lighthouse
10249 Shore Rd., Fish Creek, 920-421-3636
doorcountyhistoricalsociety.org/eagle-bluff-light-station

Kewaunee Pierhead Lighthouse
Kewaunee, 920-388-2728
kewauneepierheadlighthouse.org

North Point Lighthouse
2650 N Wahl Ave., Milwaukee, 414-332-6754
northpointlighthouse.org

Port Washington Lighthouse
311 Johnson St., Port Washington, 262-268-9150
pwhistory.org/1860-light-station

HONOR THOSE WHO SERVED
AT THE WISCONSIN VETERANS MUSEUM

With a variety of exhibits that tell the stories of Wisconsin veterans from the Civil War to the present day, this museum is a great place to learn about the history of Wisconsin's involvement in the armed forces.

Established in 1901, the current location opened in 1991 and allows visitors to see more than 2,000 artifacts ranging from the Civil War down to items from the Persian Gulf Conflict. The curators believe every veteran has a story, and they are trying to make sure that each one is told.

Catch a glimpse of what life was like for the soldiers on the front lines as well as those who served at home. From their UH-1 Iroquois "HUEY" to the amazing collection of battle flags, you will see something impressive every time you visit.

This is a must-see for anyone who wants to learn more about our state's rich military history, and the best part? It is free!

30 W Mifflin St., Madison, 608-267-1799
veterans.museum@dva.wisconsin.gov

SCOUT
THE PIONEER PARK
HISTORICAL COMPLEX

The historical complex is a unique, hidden gem located along Oneida Avenue in the south-central part of Rhinelander and is home to seven major attractions. These include the Civilian Conservation Corps barracks, the Logging Museum, a fire museum, the Restored Soo Line Depot, an antique sawmill, the Boating Museum, and a historic schoolhouse.

The Civilian Conservation Corps played an essential role in the growth of our national and state parks, and the barracks is a fascinating place to explore.

The Logging Museum is a recreation of an old logging camp, complete with a bunkhouse and cookshack, while the fire museum houses three restored fire engines, including a replica drawn by a horse. You will see so many more amazing things!

There is no charge for entry, but Pioneer Park relies on donations to operate and service the facility throughout the summer.

334 N Pelham St., Rhinelander, 715-369-5004
explorerhinelander.com

ATTEND
A WISCONSIN POWWOW

Being home to 11 different tribal nations, Wisconsin is a great place to attend a powwow and experience Native American culture. Each nation has its own specific culture and traditions. You can choose from the Bad River Band, Forest County Potawatomi, Ho-Chunk Nation, Lac Courte Oreille Band, Lac Du Flambeau Band, Menomonee Nation, Mole Lake Sokaogon Chippewa Community, Oneida Nation, Red Cliff Band, St. Croix Band, and the Stockbridge-Nunsee Band tribes.

No tribe is the same, making attending more than one powwow a great idea. In general, attendees can expect to taste amazing food, shop handmade arts and crafts, see intricate and beautiful dance performances, and listen to drummers and storytellers. It is the perfect way to learn more about the rich history of Wisconsin's Native American tribes.

Native American Tourism of Wisconsin
2932 Hwy. 47 N, Lac du Flambeau, 715-861-1212
natow.org

GENERAL POWWOW ETIQUETTE TIPS

Think of it as visiting someone's church. Use common sense, and dress and act respectfully. This is the celebration of their culture, and you are a guest.

- Never bring alcohol.
- Dress appropriately—no offensive shirts or hats.
- Don't touch the performers.
- Don't refer to their ceremonial garments or regalia as costumes. These are often handmade by the dancer wearing them.
- Ask before taking pictures of the dancers.
- Do not cross the dance grounds as a short cut, as the circles cannot be broken.
- Do not haggle with vendors. Prices are set for a reason.
- Do not sit on a bench where there is a blanket.
- Follow along with what the Master of Ceremony says.
- Stand during their National Anthem or Flag Song.
- Do not join the dance circle until you are invited to, *if* you are invited to.

FIND PAUL BUNYAN
AT THE WISCONSIN LOGGING MUSEUM

Logging was a huge part of Wisconsin's history, and this place helps to tell that story. This authentic 1890s logging camp reproduction features a variety of exhibits that covers logging in Wisconsin from the early days of log driving for over 85 years.

With things like a cook's shanty, bunkhouse, barn, and blacksmith shop, it's easy to get a feel for what life would have been like back in the day. And of course, no logging museum would be complete without a giant statue of Paul Bunyan and his big blue ox, Babe. They sit out front proudly and wait for your Instagram-able moment.

The museum also hosts the US Open Chainsaw Carving Championship! Over four days, contestants turn their eight-foot logs into roughly 150 amazing works of art that are then auctioned off as a fundraiser for the museum. It's a must-see event for any chainsaw-carving fan.

1110 E Half Moon Dr., Eau Claire, 715-835-6200
wisconsinlogging.org

LEARN
AT THE NATIONAL HISTORIC CHEESEMAKING CENTER

Located in Monroe, this is the place to go if you are curious about how over 600 types of cheese are made through a standard five-step process.

The center is located inside a rescued and renovated train depot since 1995, and you can learn how cheese has been around since the Egyptians put it into the pyramids. Next, watch a video presentation on how Wisconsin became known for its delicious cheese, then go through an authentic Farmstead Cheese Factory from the 1800s!

Learn the answers to all sorts of interesting questions—like why did a lot of small farmers stop making cheese in 1917? How much did a full milk can weigh? What did they do with the whey after they removed the curds to press? You'll even learn how the influx of Swiss settlers came into their cheesemaking heritage.

Whether you are a fan of cheddar or Swiss cheese or just love history, be sure to add the National Historic Cheesemaking Center to your itinerary.

State Rd. 69 S and 21st St., Monroe, 608-325-4636
nationalhistoriccheesemakingcenter.org

TOUR
THE GOVERNOR'S MANSION

Built in 1949, the Executive Residence has housed 15 Wisconsin governors and their families on the eastern shore of Lake Mendota. The Mansion is a Southern Classical Revival–style building with three floors and almost 20,000 square feet of room. With beautiful architectural features, including a grand staircase, fireplaces, and chandeliers, it's no wonder that it amazes the almost 20,000 people that visit or tour it for free each year.

Tours last just under an hour and are led by knowledgeable docents who have been on board for several years. They share the history of the building, information on the art and furnishings, and more in intimate groups of just a dozen people. Reservations are required on a first-come, first-served basis, and a photo ID is required for anyone over 18.

99 Cambridge Rd., Maple Bluff, 608-246-5501
wisconsinexecutiveresidence.com

TIP
Leave the large bags at home or in your car to save time during check-in.

SEE THEATER UNDER THE STARS
AT AMERICAN PLAYERS THEATER

There is nothing like sitting in an outdoor amphitheater as you watch incredibly talented actors perform amidst the sounds of nature. You aren't sitting on a picnic blanket; you are in actual seats.

Founded in 1977, the American Players Theater is home to one of the most prestigious theater companies in the US and the perfect place to see theater under the stars on a Wisconsin summer night.

Classical works from Shakespeare were the original programming, but they added several other playwrights in 1985 to help stage nine plays each year. Eight are in the summer and one is in the winter in their smaller indoor theater, allowing over 110,000 visitors a year.

Make a night out of it by packing your own picnic supper, ordering one in advance through their partner restaurant for pick up, or even grilling out on one of their many gas grills.

5950 Golf Course Rd., Spring Green, 608-588-2361
americanplayers.org

GO BACK TO KINDERGARTEN
IN WATERTOWN

At just 16 years old, Margarethe Meyer Schurz found her inspiration and calling from listening to German educator Friedrich Fröbe. Years later, living in America in 1856 after emigrating from Germany, she would create the first documented kindergarten in the US.

She started with five pupils in her own home, and soon her school was growing to the point that she had to move it to its own building in town to accommodate all the students. It would remain open until the anti-German feelings during WWI closed it.

The building itself would change a lot, serving as a cigar factory, fish store, and religious bookstore until it was about to be destroyed. In 1956, it was saved, moved next to the Octagon House Museum, and restored by the Watertown Historical Society.

919 Charles St., Watertown, 920-261-2796
octagonhousemuseum.org/first

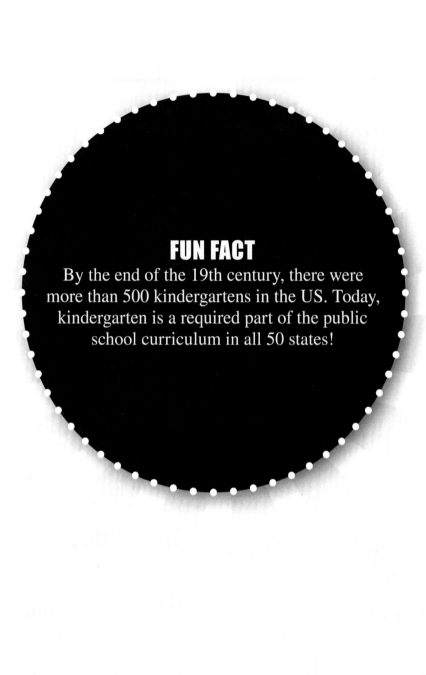

FUN FACT

By the end of the 19th century, there were more than 500 kindergartens in the US. Today, kindergarten is a required part of the public school curriculum in all 50 states!

GO THROUGH
THE MILWAUKEE ART MUSEUM

You can't miss the iconic building on the shores of Lake Michigan that houses the Milwaukee Art Museum (MAM). With four floors and over 40 galleries, they have plenty of space to display everything from classic paintings from masters such as Rembrandt and Monet to modern sculptures by artists like Henry Moore and Barbara Hepworth. One highlight is the impressive collection of works from Sun Prairie, Wisconsin, native Georgia O'Keefe.

In addition to its many extensive permanent collections, the Milwaukee Art Museum also hosts temporary exhibitions from across the globe. These collections are constantly changing, so make sure to check out their website to see what is currently available.

Events are back in the Lakeside at MAM program, and if you have littles, make sure to visit the Kohl's Art Studio for hands-on (and educational) fun.

700 N Art Museum Dr., Milwaukee, 414-224-3220
mam.org

TIP
Bring your earbuds to listen to museum audio guides on your smartphone as you tour MAM.

PAY YOUR RESPECTS
TO KATE BLOOD

Appleton is home to Riverside Cemetery, one of the oldest cemeteries in the state. Within that cemetery is the final resting place of Kate Blood.

Kate's grave has become a popular attraction for tourists and history buffs. The terrifying tale behind this tombstone begins with the grave's disquieting location on the river.

According to rumors, Kate Blood killed her husband and three children before committing suicide. Other tales say that anybody who approaches her tomb under a full moon can see blood dripping from the face of the family stone bearing her name.

The reality, however, is far more prosaic and less enchanting. Kate did not commit any murders and passed away before her husband (though not by his hand). She contracted tuberculosis at 23 and had to move south for a warmer environment.

She passed away in Lawrence, Kansas, and a train delivered her body home. Today, Kate's grave is separated from the rest of Riverside Cemetery, set atop a hill near the Fox River.

714 N Owaissa St., Appleton, 920-733-5629
riversidecemeteryappleton.com

EXPERIENCE
THE WEGNER GROTTO

Nestled among the rolling hills of the Driftless Region, the Wegner Grotto was built in 1931 by German immigrants Paul and Matilda Wegner.

They were inspired to create their sculpture garden out of concrete and broken glass after an inspiring visit to the Dickeyville Grotto. The result is an impressive and unique display of religious icons, patriotic symbols, and nature scenes. It's truly a sight to behold and something you won't find anywhere else in the world.

The Wegners started with the ship that brought them to America, the *Bremen*, and went from there until their last piece—the replica of their 50th wedding anniversary cake.

The shining star is the glass church, which has hosted several weddings. It's a beautiful and serene spot that is definitely worth a visit.

While the Wegner Grotto is free to visit, it is only open from Memorial Day through Labor Day.

7788 Daylight Rd., Sparta, 608-269-8680
mclhr.org/wegnergrotto.php

VISIT
THE APOSTLE ISLANDS NATIONAL LAKESHORE

With 21 different islands, 19 of which you can camp on, you can experience 12 miles of mainland coast on Lake Superior.

This National Recreation Area has nine lighthouses over six islands and an impressive array of both rock formations and sea caves.

The Apostle Islands National Lakeshore offers a little bit of everything for the outdoor enthusiast. With kayaking, camping, hiking, and climbing, there isn't much of the area that you can't experience.

One thing to remember is that these are situated on one of the great lakes. You need to be aware of the weather if you plan to get yourself there under your own paddle power.

When winter comes, the Apostle Islands are transformed into a winter wonderland, with ice caves that are sure to take your breath away, which are fairly easy to navigate if you have the proper footwear.

nps.gov/apis/index.htm

EXPERIENCE STEM
AT THE ATLAS SCIENCE CENTER

Formerly the Paper Discovery Center, the Atlas Science Center is still a must-visit for anyone interested in the science and technology of papermaking.

Housed in the former Atlas paper mill, the center now offers even more interactive exhibits that are perfect for all ages. You can explore the science of sound, experiment with different types of energy, and even make your own paper!

They have an entire room dedicated to understanding the importance of recycling and how to do it correctly. One entire wall shows eco-friendly swap-outs for common daily items. The collection of photos that showcases people with just one week of their garbage is jaw-dropping.

Time your visit to be able to take part in their "Survival" game show. It is a fun yet educational activity for the entire family. You will be tasked with completing different challenges that will teach you more about people, the planet, and prosperity.

425 W Water St., Appleton, 920-380-7491
atlassciencecenter.org

TOUR
A CRANBERRY MARSH

While most people know Wisconsin as the dairy state, it is also one of the top producers of cranberries in the US. Cranberries are native to North America and have been cultivated in Wisconsin for over 150 years.

Today, there are over 250 cranberry growers in Wisconsin, and the state produces about 62 percent of the nation's annual harvest.

If you want to look like the guys in the Ocean Spray commercial, complete with waders and standing in a cranberry bog, then this is for you! You can have a lot of fun and learn about a 100-year-old family-run business as you dine out of food trucks, listen to live music, and more.

The August wagon tours are only $15; the fun photo opportunity costs $75, and is usually only one weekend in October.

1060 Center St., Wisconsin Rapids, 715-544-7438
rootedinred.co

Create Custom Scents at the Candle Mercantile (page 150)

SHOPPING AND FASHION

CREATE CUSTOM SCENTS
AT THE CANDLE MERCANTILE

Looking for a unique store that creates a one-of-a-kind experience? This farm-chic treasure is it!

Candles, wax tarts, reed diffusers, or even room sprays can be created with your own custom-made scent!

You start by choosing from over 90 different non-synthetic, high-quality fragrances. Don't be overwhelmed, as the staff has magical ways to help you narrow things down to create the perfect combination for you.

Once you have your scent, then you pick your vessel, and finally you choose whether you want a wooden wick or a regular wick.

Plan ahead: The entire process takes about an hour, and then roughly another 90 minutes to "cure" before you take it home. You will want to do this earlier in the day so you can enjoy a little more of Lake Geneva before you pick your wonderful creation up.

870 W Main St., Lake Geneva, 262-203-5557
thecandlemercantile.com

TIP
Phone first to make sure they have space at the creation bar.

GET YOUR GOAT MILK PRODUCT FIX
AT FLOPPY EAR FARM

Wisconsin is quickly becoming America's dairy-goat-land as more dairy goat farms in Wisconsin have cropped up in recent years. There is nothing better for Wisconsin winter skin than goat's milk soap or lotion!

Floppy Ear Farm is the place to shop, with their impressive line of National Award-Winning goat milk body care products.

While their 46-acre farm is home to their goats, they sell most of their products online or at events like the Sheboygan Farmers Market.

Goat milk products are becoming more and more popular as people learn about the benefits of using them. From bath bombs and fizzies to dog shampoo bars, they have thought of almost everything you can make out of goat's milk. I was impressed with their haircare line, and they even make powdered laundry detergent!

16711 Hilltop Rd., Reedsville, 920-775-9364
floppyearfarm.com

SUPPORT WOMEN
AT ADORN OF JANESVILLE

When Margie Siggelkow opened Adorn in 2019, her goal was to include as many ethically sourced items as possible. She found woman-owned companies in the US and beyond to make that happen in her own community.

Instead of complaining about what was missing, she opened a store that she would love to go to herself—and she keeps that vision in mind as she goes forward.

From jewelry to artisan note cards to ethically made, zero-waste fashions, Adorn has pretty much everything you could need—and if they don't have it, they will try to find it or direct you where you can get it.

When women support other women, good things happen in the world, and Margie is doing her best to help with that!

Check out Adorn next time you are in Janesville, Wisconsin, or visit her online shop.

39 S Main St., Janesville, 608-563-0913
adornjanesville.com

CHECK OUT
THE POTTER'S SHED

In Shell Lake you will find a unique and welcoming complex that is the home to seven different businesses.

Starting with wholesale pottery in the early 90s, they now include a beautiful gallery to shop from that houses the work of over 200 artists from the US and Canada, a cafe with homemade food, a paint-your-own pottery studio, a consignment store, and an online store, and they host live music outdoors.

It is truly a blend of family passions, and you can feel it as you walk through on your visit.

Over the years, this family-run company has amassed a fantastic team of workers who always think of innovative methods to draw customers to their establishment. So, when you are ready to explore, stop by and see why this unique place is one of northern Wisconsin's top destinations!

260 Industrial Blvd., Shell Lake, 715-468-4122
thepottersshed.com

TIP

If you are there with the littles, check out the Fairy Door Hunt!

BUY WISCONSIN VODKA
AT PERLICK DISTILLERY

Sorry Russia, we have amazing vodka made right here in Wisconsin and it can be found at Perlick Distillery.

This family-owned business makes their spirits from ingredients they grow on their own farm. This helps them keep things simple and make sure that what they do, they do very well.

Keeping it simple for them means they do not have a food menu, but instead have partnered with a local restaurant to deliver a variety of stone-fired pizzas and shareables. Food is important when you spend a little time in their tasting room.

That tasting room is incredible! They can accommodate 250 people between indoor and outdoor seating. Notice the beautiful hardwood that came from their own farm. Scott also laid the field rock floor himself—after cutting it all into two-inch stubs.

The result? Amazing craft cocktails in a beautiful and friendly environment. I highly recommend the "Lemon Drop."

W5150 County Hwy. B, Sarona, 715-296-5087
perlickdistillery.com

TIP
Plan your visit for the first two weeks
in August to go through their sunflower maze.

GET ORNAMENTS
AT THE KRISTMAS KRINGLE SHOPPE

The Kristmas Kringle Shoppe is a must-see stop in Wisconsin! This unique shop offers a wide variety of Christmas ornaments, ranging from collectible Old World Ornaments to Department 56. They even keep a calligrapher on staff to help personalize the ornaments you purchase with impeccable handwriting.

They have over 70 themed trees to peruse, along with anything you need for that Christmas Village you display or to finish off your Nativity set. You can choose from an incredible variety of other holiday decorations, including trees, wreaths, stockings, and more.

Whether you're looking for the perfect ornament to add to your collection or a unique gift for someone special, the Kristmas Kringle Shoppe has made a point to be sure to have what you're looking for. Since 1978, they have offered a wide range of prices, so you can find something to fit any budget. And if you can't make it to the store, they also offer an online shop for your convenience.

1330 S Main St., Fond du Lac, 920-922-3900
kristmaskringle.com

GRAB YOUR BADGERS GEAR
AT THE UW BOOKSTORE

As any true Wisconsinite knows, there is no greater feeling than cheering on the Badgers on a crisp fall day. Whether you are headed to Camp Randall or watching the game from home, you will want to ensure you are decked out in your best Badgers fan gear.

The University of Wisconsin Bookstore is the perfect place to find what you need to support your team. From T-shirts and hats to sweatshirts and jackets, the UW Bookstore has everything you need to show your Badgers pride.

They also carry a great selection of novelty items, like the temporary tattoos and foam fingers that students love. They also offer mugs, keychains, phone cases, and shot glasses.

So, whether you are looking for the perfect gift for a fellow fan or just treating yourself, this is the place to stop. Go Bucky!

711 State St., Madison, 608-257-3784
uwbookstore.com

Get Your Frank Lloyd Wright Fix at Taliesin (page 120)

ACTIVITIES
BY SEASON

WINTER

SPRING

• •

SUMMER

FALL

• •

Ride the Original Wisconsin Ducks (page 46)

Admire the Woodwork at the Paine Art Center (page 122)

SUGGESTED
ITINERARIES

ART AND ARCHITECTURE

Hang with Your Peeps at the Racine Art Museum, 40

Experience the House on the Rock, 43

See Folk Art at Fred Smith's Concrete Park, 58

Go through the Milwaukee Art Museum, 142

Escape to the Mitchell Park Domes of Milwaukee, 44

Learn about the Wisconsin State Capitol Building, 110

Get Your Frank Lloyd Wright Fix at Taliesin, 120

Admire the Woodwork at the Paine Art Center, 122

Experience the Wegner Grotto, 144

Dig Up Cornish History at Pendarvis, 126

FESTIVALS

Get a Wisconsin State Fair Cream Puff, 21

Go Medieval at the Bristol Renaissance Faire, 36

Throw Cow Poop in Prairie du Sac, 104

Enjoy an Out-of-This-World Celebration in Elmwood, 54

Rock Out at Milwaukee's Summerfest, 56

Spear a Sturgeon, 73

Attend a Wisconsin Powwow, 134

• •

OUTDOOR ADVENTURES

FAMILY FUN

DATE NIGHT

HISTORY LESSONS

• •

Eat under the Goats at Al Johnson's (page 10)

INDEX

• •

• •

• •

• •

Experience Luxury at Villa Louis (page 128)